Knotted Lace

MILNER CRAFT SERIES

Knotted Lace

ELENA DICKSON

SALLY MILNER PUBLISHING

First published in 1992 by
Sally Milner Publishing Pty Ltd
67 Glassop Street
Birchgrove NSW 2041 Australia

Reprinted in 1992

Production by Sylvana Scannapiego,
Island Graphics
Design by David Constable
Layout Gatya Kelly, Doric Order
Colour photography by Andre Martin
Black & white photography by Steve Williams
and Michael Bambacas
Typeset in Australia by Asset Typesetting Pty Ltd
Printed in Australia by Impact Printing, Melbourne

National Library of Australia
Cataloguing-in-Publication data:

Dickson, Elena.
   Knotted lace

   ISBN 1 86351 055 9.

   1. Lace and lacemaking. I. Title.

746.22

Distributed in Australia by Transworld Publishers

DEDICATION

This book is dedicated to the memory of my mother-in-law, Eirene Dimetriou Dickson, who shared with me her love of this beautiful needle lace.

The Author

Elena Dickson's interests in handwork began at the age of eight, and her mother, a skilled needlewoman, fostered this talent. When Elena married, her Greek mother-in-law introduced her to the art of making knotted lace, or dandella. In 1987 she began to teach this ancient skill to members of the South Australian branch of the Australian Lace Guild and she has continued to give lessons in this form of lace making.

Elena lives with her husband and three sons in Adelaide.

CONTENTS

ACKNOWLEDGEMENTS

So many people have given me their help and support during the writing of this book and I would very much like to express my sincere appreciation for their efforts.

Firstly to my son Alex for his help with the computer and for adapting my diagrams, and to my niece Eran Svigos for her excellent drawing skills.

Also to Steve Williams and Michael Bambacas for their expertise and the time they spent taking the beautiful photographs for my book.

My thanks also to Salwa Jubrail Urch and Nina Jubrail, as well as the Dickson and Bambacas families for allowing me to examine, photograph and use their mothers' designs. To Angelliky Topalsavas and Katerina Mourcella, thank you for allowing me to photograph and use your designs.

For the Arabic names and their translations my thanks to Adele Jubrail Crawford.

Without the prompting and encouragement from the ladies of my first lace class, this book would still be a pile of notes, so to Audrey McKenzie, Jean Lange, Anky Vel, Lyn Branson, and the late Jean Strath, thank you for your suggestions and for finding the errors in my first working notes. Thanks also to my dear friend Lynne Webbe for her proof-reading skills.

Last, but certainly not least, my love and thanks to my family for their love and consideration during the many hours I spent working on the samplers and writing the text.

Elena Dickson, 1991.

PREFACE

In 1926, a migrant ship arrived in Australia. On board were 60 women from the island of Kastellorizo, a small Greek island situated off the coast of Turkey. Many of the younger women had come to meet and marry the men chosen to be their husbands. Along with their hopes for a happier and more successful future, they brought with them trunks containing items of household linen for their new homes. As was the custom at this time, most of this linen was handmade and decorated with a variety of different handwork including embroidery, crochet and dandella — a beautiful, yet durable knotted lace. More importantly, many brought with them their skill and knowledge of how to make this lace.

I became interested in this beautiful lace and was fortunate to learn how to make it when I married. My mother-in-law, Eirene Dimetriou Dickson, was one of the young girls who came from Kastellorizo, Greece. She had become expert at making this lace when she was only eight years old. From this early age she and her elder sister Flora would rise at 5 am each morning and work on a variety of lace and needlework until midday. These items were traded with Turkish and Cypriot merchants to help supplement the family income. It was not until their family came to Adelaide that the girls were able to begin work on various items for their own trousseaux. Although my mother-in-law was skilled in many forms of handwork she much preferred making this intricate lace and she continued to do so right up to her death in 1988. Over the years she made countless beautiful doilies which she gave to her children and grandchildren.

My decision to write this book resulted from my inability to find written instructions on how to work many of the traditional designs. I was taught in the traditional way, that is by example. However, as the years went by I found that my mother-in-law, as well as her friends, were forgetting how they had worked their more intricate patterns. Many of these women are now in their late seventies and eighties, or have passed away, without passing on their skill. They have never used written instructions as they either created their own designs or copied them from the work of their friends and relatives. Written instructions would not have been of much use to many women of their generation, particularly those of the Moslem countries, as most were illiterate. Hopefully, with this book their skills will not be forgotten.

Dandella or Eastern Mediterranean knotted lace is a simple needle lace where a knot is used to make loops of different size, shape and length. Intricate patterns are created by combining these loops in a variety of ways. Although there are many traditional designs, the number of different pattern combinations is limited only by your imagination and creative ability. Once the knot has been mastered all that is required is to maintain an even tension. Despite its delicate appearance this lace is very durable and easily laundered. Silk, linen and cotton threads can be used to make doilies as well as edgings for clothing and household items such as bed linen, curtains, tablecloths and handkerchiefs.

From the very few references I have been able to find on this craft, I am still unable to pinpoint exactly where it originated. It can be found in many areas of Greece, particularly the islands of Kastellorizo (now known as Megisti), Naxos, Rhodes and Crete. And it can also be found in Cyprus, Turkey, Palestine, Armenia and Lebanon. Naturally, all of these countries claim it as their own. However, as some scholars believe that this lace dates back to the time of the Phoenicians, it is safe to assume that it originated in the Eastern Mediterranean and has spread throughout the region in the same way as the similarities in the cultures and cuisines of these countries.

This lacework is known by a variety of names. It is commonly referred to as Armenian lace, but is also known as Rodi lace, Nazareth lace, Phoenician lace, Palestinian lace, Smyrna stitch and bibilla. In the Greek language *bibilla* is the term used for any small or delicate lace edging. However, in Cyprus, and in many of the Moslem countries, it is the name of the technique used to make delicate flowers and leaves of this knotted lace. These flowers were usually worked around the edges of the headscarves worn by Moslem women, or fashioned into garlands to be used as collars.

The Greek name for this lace is *dandella tes velonas* (lace of the needle) or *kombo velonya* (knotted needlework). In Arabic it is referred to as *ajour el Nasrah* (lace of Nazareth). Unfortunately, many of the elderly Greek women I interviewed could not remember, or did not know, the names of many of the different patterns they had worked. In order to identify the patterns in this book I have taken the liberty of inventing suitable names where I could not find a traditional one. My Palestinian friends were able to find the Arabic names for some of the patterns; therefore, I have included those, as well as the few Greek names I did find, at the beginning of each pattern.

GLOSSARY

As I have been unable to find any traditional terms for these knotted lace techniques, I have taken the liberty of inventing some which will make my written instructions easier to follow.

BASIC LOOPS

Uniformly sized and spaced loops.

BRIDGING LOOPS

A small loop worked into a large or small loop which is not worked into on the next round or row.

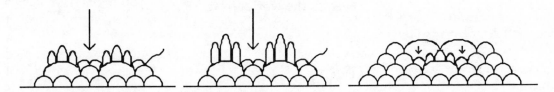

CLOSED LOOPS

A knot that is worked into the top of the last loop worked.

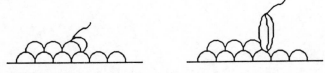

LARGE LOOPS

Loops made by missing one or more basic loops.

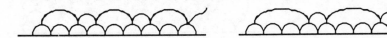

LONG OR SHORT LOOPS

Loops of larger than normal size worked into a basic or large loop.

FOUNDATION ROUND OR ROW

The round or row of basic loops on which a pattern will be worked.

Note: When working a foundation round, always make the loops in multiples required for the next pattern. I have given directions for multiples where necessary. For circular designs, these loops can be smaller and closer together as they will spread and become more even as the work grows.

PICOTS

A series of small loops made into a basic or large loop.

RAISED STITCH

The technique used to make a filled design.

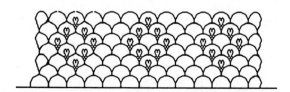

SIDE STITCH

A small closed loop followed by a large loop. The large loop can be worked into the same loop, or the loop next to the closed loop.

SMALL TURNING LOOP

A loop used to turn work when working on the straight. This loop is *not* worked into each row.

TURNING LOOP

A stitch used to turn work when working on the straight. This loop *must be* worked into each row to keep the edges straight.

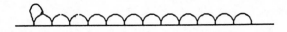

MATERIALS AND EQUIPMENT

This is a very economical craft as the equipment necessary to make the lace are items found in most homes. All that is required is:

- A No 3 darning needle or a No 3 straw needle.
- Thread — twisted cotton thread such as Coats or DMC Mercerized crochet cotton. Best results are achieved with the Greek Butterfly crochet cotton No 50.
- Scissors — small, sharp embroidery scissors.
- Small safety pins (optional). Useful when counting loops or marking the beginning of rounds.

USING THIS BOOK

My diagrams aim to make the instructions easier to follow. However, as some of the patterns are difficult to draw exactly and may appear confusing, always refer to the photograph of the sampler. And, of course, the diagram will be easier to follow if you read the instructions *prior to starting*.

For ease and convenience, all drawings show only a straight section of the workings, and so that the diagrams look balanced in themselves, some instructions start part of the way into a line, not at the beginning of the line. The dots on the foundation rows indicate the pattern repeats. Commonsense and some other craft ability will help you read the diagrams.

CHAPTER ONE

STITCHES AND PATTERNS

BASIC LOOPS

Basic loops are the small evenly spaced loops used in the majority of patterns. Their traditional names in Greek are *sesame* (sesame seeds) or *fasolakia* (little beans), and in Arabic, *sadaf* (shell).

Before attempting any of the samplers in the following chapters it is advisable to practise the basic loops, either on a scrap of fabric or on a small circle of fabric. Do not be discouraged if your first attempts are very uneven. The more loops you make, the better they will become.

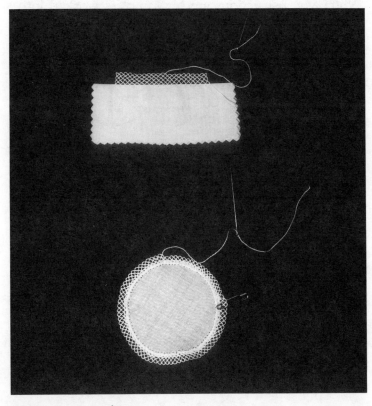

Basic Loop Samplers
Top: Basic loops worked on the straight edge of fabric
Bottom: Basic loops worked on a circle of fabric

Always work from *left* to *right* when working on a straight edge (unless you are left-handed, in which case see the instructions given later in this chapter). Make approximately 25 loops, then turn the work. Work a turning loop into the first loop and a basic loop into each loop of the previous row.

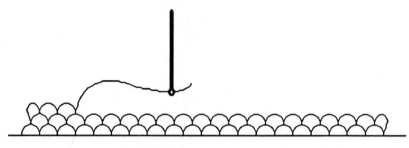

Basic Loops

When working on a circle of fabric, it is advisable to neaten the edges before beginning the lace. Again you will be working from *left* to *right*. However, it is not necessary to turn the work. When you come around to the first loop work into it in order to begin the next round.

Note: My instructions are for samplers worked into a circle of fabric approximately 6 cm (2¼″) in diameter.

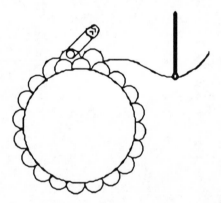

To Work a Basic Loop

- Thread needle with a length of thread approximately 60 cm (23½″) long. A longer thread may be used once you become more proficient.
- With the thread behind the fabric, hold the work between the thumb and forefinger of your left hand. Insert the needle into the fabric, 2 mm (¹⁄₁₆″) from the edge, and under the thread.

Note: Do not pull through.

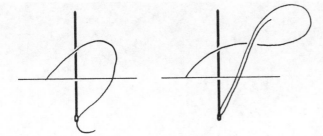

Basic Loop

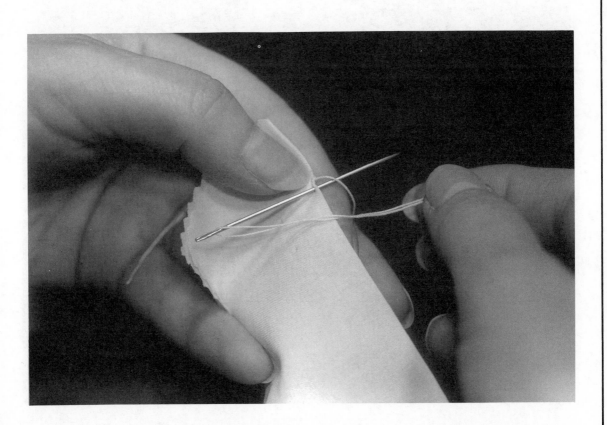

- Grasp both threads from the eye end of the needle and loop them under the point of the needle, from *right* to *left*, and down towards the eye of the needle.

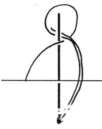

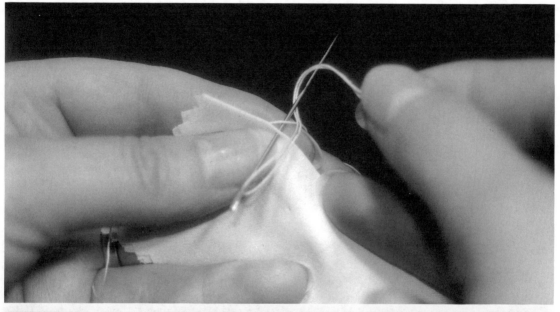

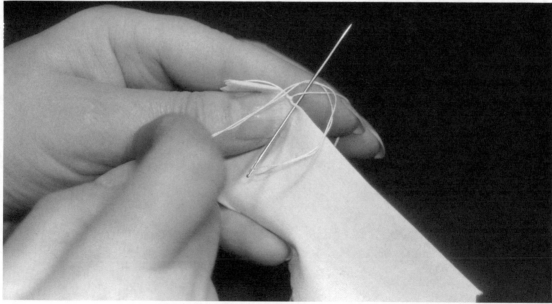

- Pull the needle through the fabric in an upwards direction, and pull the knot tight.

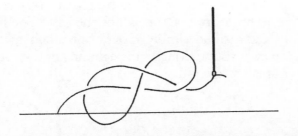

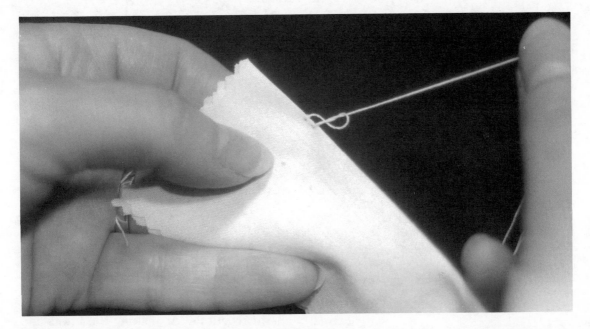

- Insert the needle 2 mm (¹⁄₁₆″) from the first knot and repeat the stitch, leaving a loop about 2 mm (¹⁄₁₆″) high. Continue in this manner until the round is complete.

Note: Do not cut thread.

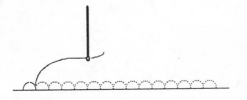

- The next round is worked in the same way, with the needle being placed into the loops of the previous round. Continue to work into the first loop of the previous round. It will appear that you are making an extra loop, but this is not the case. The first loop of each round simply moves one stitch to the right on each round. Mark the beginning of the round with a small safety pin.

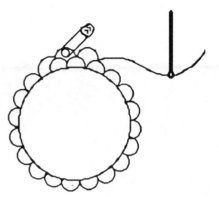

INSTRUCTIONS FOR LEFT-HANDED WORKERS

Left-handed workers will find it easier to work from *right* to *left*. The instructions for making the knots and basic loops are exactly the same as those for right-handed workers, except that the working thread passes under the point of the needle from left to right.

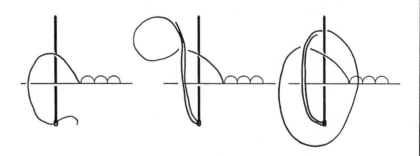

Basic Loop Stitch for Left-handed Workers

JOINING THREAD

Cut thread approximately 5 cm (2″) from the last knot worked. Over this knot make another with new thread. Work into the next loop, catching the cut end of the previous thread with the knot. This will make a double loop. Keep the thread ends at the back of the work. On the next round, work into the double loop before trimming the thread ends.

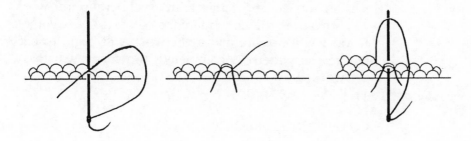

Joining Thread

INCREASING AND DECREASING

If the foundation rows or rounds are correct, it should not be necessary to increase or decrease when working a pattern. If, however, more loops are required, then increase by working two knots into one loop.

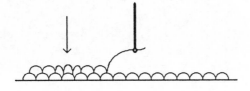

Increasing

To decrease, simply miss one loop (1), or insert the needle through two loops and make one knot (2).

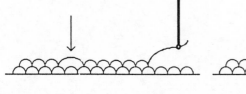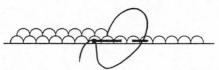

Decreasing

FOUNDATION ROUNDS OR ROWS

When beginning a new pattern, it is always advisable to work the first or foundation round in the multiples of loops required to make the pattern. Increasing or decreasing loops midway through a pattern looks untidy and spoils the look of the finished article. Counting is easier if small safety pins are used to mark the number of loops worked as you progress. When working in a circular pattern, the foundation loops can be slightly smaller and closer together than usual because the work will spread as the circumference of the work enlarges. If too few loops are made, the work will begin to curl before the pattern is completed; too many will make the work frilly.

CORRECTING ERRORS

Providing the knots are pulled tight, the lacework is impossible to undo. All errors have to be cut away. Cut through the loops and use the point of your needle to loosen the knots. It may be possible to loosen the occasional knot if it has not yet been pulled tight.

LARGE LOOP AND PICOT PATTERN
WITH LARGE LOOP AND PICOT EDGING

The traditional Greek name for large loops and picots is *handrakia* (little beads or pearls) and the Arabic name is *Shama'el assel* (beeswax). Large loop and picot edging is known as *tahlab* (moss) in Arabic.

Worked in Butterfly crochet cotton No 50.
Finished width: 3.5 cm (1⅓″).

Large Loop and Picot Pattern with Large Loop and Picot Edging

TO WORK THE LARGE LOOP AND PICOT PATTERN

First work a foundation round in a multiple of two, plus one extra loop. Work six rounds of basic loops.

- Make a round of large loops by working into every second loop.

Large Loop and Picot Pattern

- Into each of the large loops, make three small loops (picots).

- Weave the working thread through the first two picots of the first set of picots and work a knot into the middle one. Work a round of large loops, making the knots into each middle picot.

- Repeat the two previous rounds twice.
- Onto the large loops of the last round work a foundation round in a multiple of three.

- Work seven rounds of basic loops.

TO WORK THE LARGE LOOP AND PICOT EDGING

A multiple of three is required.

- Work one loop, bridge to the next basic loop and make three long picots into this loop. Repeat to the end of round.

Large Loop and Picot Edging

- Working into the basic loops between the picots, make a round of large loops.

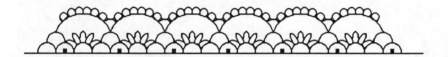

- Work six or seven very small picots into each large loop. Trim thread close to knot to finish work.

CLOSED LOOP AND BOW PATTERN
WITH CLOSED LOOP SHELL EDGING

Our name for this pattern comes from the Greek name for it — *fyongo* which means bow.

Worked in Butterfly crochet cotton No 50.
Finished width: 2.5 cm (1″).

Closed Loop and Bow Pattern with Closed Loop Shell Edging

TO WORK A CLOSED LOOP AND BOW PATTERN

Work a foundation round in a multiple of two. Work six rounds of basic loops.

- Bridge into the first loop and make a long loop, one and a half sizes longer than the basic loop. Place the needle through the front of the loop.

  Note: Do not pull through.

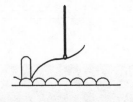 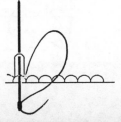

Closed Loop and Bow Pattern

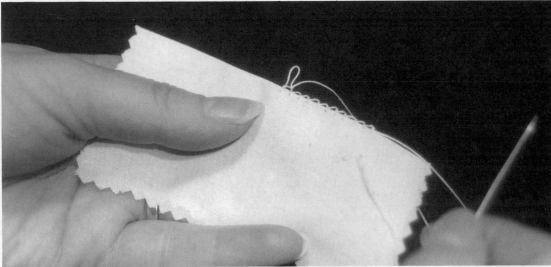

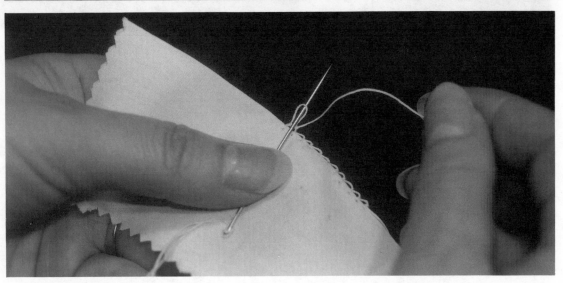

● Taking the thread from the knot end, pass it over the point of the needle from *left* to *right*, and pull the needle through. This makes a knot at the top of the loop. (Closed loop made.)

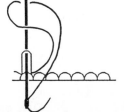 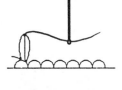

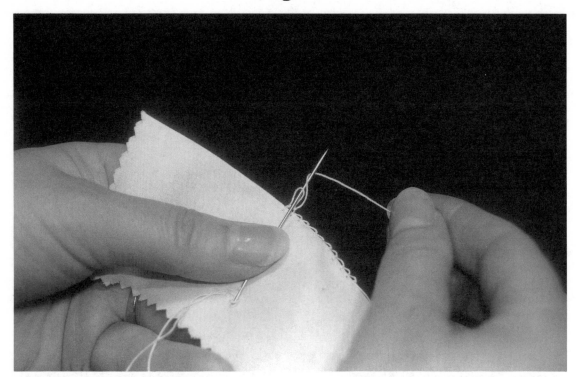

- Make another loop of the same length into the next basic loop.

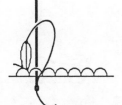 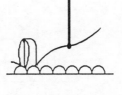

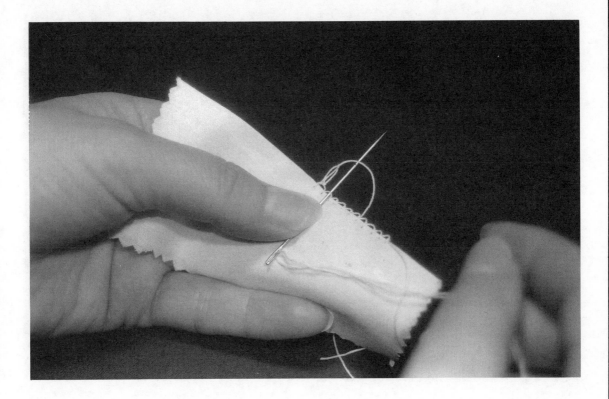

• Insert the needle behind all of the long loops and pass the thread over the needle, as in the second step. Pull all threads tight together in the middle.

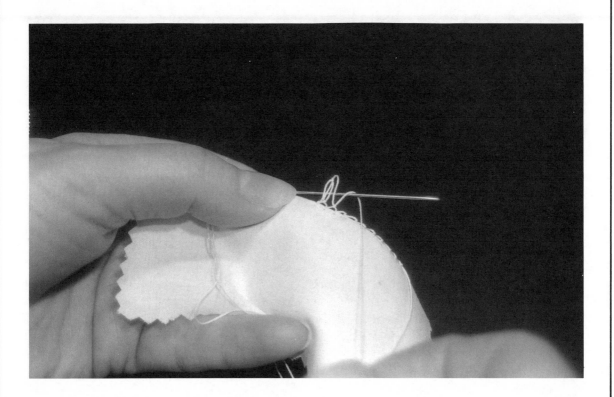

- Place the needle at the top of the last long loop and make a closed loop knot to finish the bow.

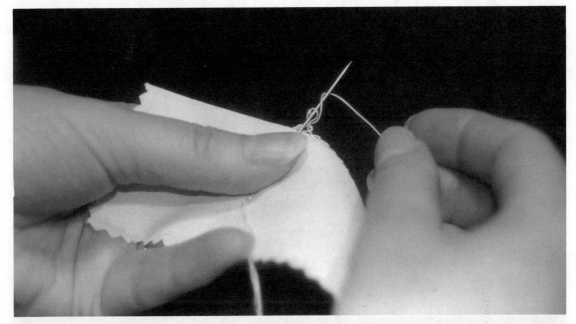

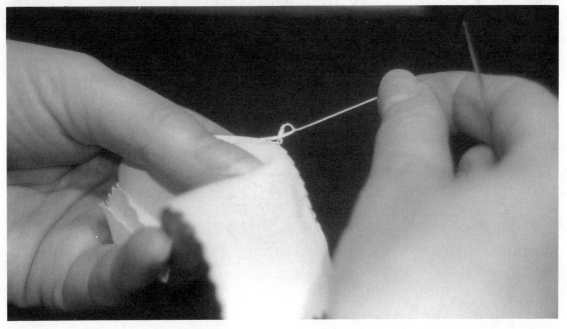

- Continue to make the bows in this manner, omitting the first step.

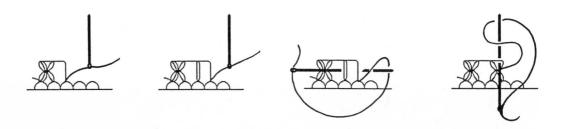

INSTRUCTIONS FOR LEFT-HANDED WORKERS

Follow the steps for right-handed workers but work from *right* to *left*. To close the loops, the thread passes over and under the needle from *right* to *left*.

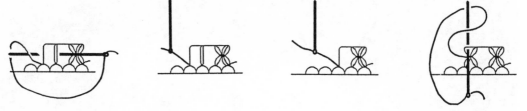

Closed Loop and Bow Pattern for Left-handed Workers

JOINING THREAD

When joining a new thread, make a knot over the last knot made into the basic loop of the previous round. Catch the end of the new thread with the knot when closing the loop. The end of the old thread can be caught with the next knot.

Joining Thread

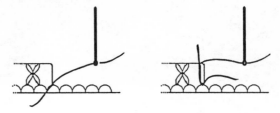

PLATE 1

TRAY CLOTH, NAPKIN, DOILY AND JUG COVER

PLATE 2

BRIDAL ACCESSORIES

PLATE 3

CUSHION AND GIFT ITEMS

PLATE 4

GIRL'S DRESS COLLAR, CHRISTENING GOWN AND BABY'S BIB

PLATE 5

COLLAR, HANDKERCHIEF, TRAY CLOTH, JAR COVER AND SACHETS

PLATE 6

DOLL'S THINGS

PLATE 7
PINCUSHION WITH UNFINISHED HANDKERCHIEF AND
SQUARE DOILY

PLATE 1

Tray cloth can be made by working steps one to eleven, and the 'Filled lattice edging' of the Oval Doily in Chapter 6;

Table napkin is edged with the 'Closed loop shell edging' in Chapter 1;

Round Doily instructions can be found in Chapter 6;

Milk jug cover is made by adding glass beads to the ends of the 'Knotted rose ground' sampler in Chapter 1.

PLATE 2

Coathanger is edged with the 'Floral fan edging; in Chapter 4;

Heart bridal charm is trimmed with a 'Tufted picot fan edging' described in Chapter 1;

Handkerchief features the 'Large loop and picot corner with feathered picot fan edging' which is in Chapter 5;

Lace mat is made by working the 'Picot lattice pattern with a fancy closed loop scallop edging' in Chapter 5;

Silver frame contains the 'Long loop medallion' from Chapter 3'

Garter is worked following the instructions for the 'Basic fan edging' in Chapter 1, however the 'Side stitch pattern', Chapter 1, is substituted for the long loops and picots.

PLATE 3

Blue cushion features the Square Doily described in Chapter 6;

Soap bag has the 'Bibilla flower' from Chapter 3 stitched onto the front, and is trimmed with the edging found in the 'Spiral motif' in Chapter 3;

Purse tissue cover has a row of 'Bows' from the 'Bow pattern' in Chapter 1 as a ribbon insertion and is trimmed with the 'Side stitch edging' from Chapter 1;

Bookmark is edged with a 'Fancy closed loop and picot scollop edging' from Chapter 5;

Glass paper weight contains the 'Long loop medallion' from Chapter 3.

PLATE 4

Girls' dress collar is the Lace Collar featured in Chapter 6;

Christening gown is trimmed with the 'Fancy closed loop and picot scollop edging' from Chapter 5;

Baby's bib is edged with the 'Basic fan edging' from Chapter 1.

PLATE 5

False collar is trimmed with the 'Large loop and picot edging' found in Chapter 1;

Handkerchief is made by working the 'Three picot corner with closed loop and picot fan edging' from Chapter 5;

Tray cloth is trimmed with the 'Flower edging' from Chapter 4;

Jar cover has a ribbon threaded through the first row of large loops of the 'Large loop and picot' sampler in Chapter 1;

Round lavender sachet is made by working the first six steps of the 'Spiral motif' in Chapter 3. 'Bows' from Chapter 1 form the ribbon insertion. Finished with three rows of 'Basic loops' and 'Free pineapple edging' from Chapter 1;

Square lavender sachet is made by working the 'Butterfly design', from the Square Doily in Chapter 6, on 21 basic loops. 'Bows' have been used as a ribbon insertion and the edging is a 'Pyramid pattern' from Chapter 1 topped with the 'Floral fan edging' from Chapter 4.

PLATE 6

Doll's bedspread is made by working the 'Picot lattice pattern' in Chapter 5 and edged with the 'Bow and picot edging' in Chapter 4;

Chair back is made by working the first and last pattern repeats of the Diamond Design Bookmark in chapter 6;

Cushion motif is made by working one 'Centre motif' of the Oval Doily in Chapter 6.

PLATE 7

Pin cushion bracelet features the 'Large loop and picot medallion' from Chapter 3 and is edged with the same large loop and picot edging that surrounds the medallion;

Unfinished handkerchief features the 'Bell stitch pattern' from Chapter 5;

Unfinished square doily has a 'Picot lattice pattern' centre from Chapter 5 with 'Basic loops' and 'Bows' surrounding it.

TO WORK CLOSED LOOP SHELL EDGING

On top of bows, work a foundation round in a multiple of seven. Work six rounds of basic loops.

- Miss one loop by working a large loop into the following loop. Make five basic loops. Repeat to the end of the round.

Closed Loop Shell Edging

- Missing the basic loops either side of the large loop, work four long closed loops into the large loop. (Second step of bows). Work two basic loops. Repeat to the end of the round.

- Into the first large loop, work a small picot and a long picot twice. Work a small and a long picot into the next three loops. Make a small picot and a long picot, twice, into the next large loop. Bridge into the next basic loop and work one basic loop. Repeat to the end of round. Trim the thread close to the knot to finish off work.

PYRAMID PATTERN
WITH BIBILLA PYRAMID EDGING

The traditional Greek name for the Pyramid pattern is *pyramida*, and the Arabic is *ahramet ma'breem* (pyramids with lace). The edging is known as *kombo bibilla* (knotted edging) or *pyramides* (pyramids) in Greek, and *ahram* (pyramids) in Arabic.

Worked in Butterfly crochet cotton No 50.
Finished width: 2.5 cm (1″).

Pyramid Pattern with Bibilla Pyramid Edging

TO WORK THE PYRAMID PATTERN

Work a foundation round in a multiple of five and work two rounds of basic loops.

- Miss one loop by working a large loop into the following loop. Work three basic loops. Repeat to the end of the round.

Pyramid Pattern

- Miss the large loop each round, making it longer each time. The basic loops will decrease by one each round.

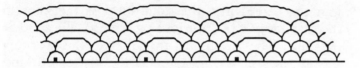

- Onto the large loops between the pyramids, work a foundation round in a multiple of five.
- Work six rounds of basic loops.

TO WORK THE BIBILLA PYRAMID EDGING

A multiple of five is required.

- Work five basic loops.

Bibilla Pyramid Edging

- Turn work and make a large loop into the first loop. Turn work.

- Work four basic loops, catching the large loop of previous round with each knot.

- Repeat the second and third steps, decreasing one loop each row, until one loop remains. Work a knot into the one remaining loop. Turn the work and work small basic loops along the edge of the pyramid, towards the bottom of the first loop. Pull the thread tight and trim close to the knot.

- Join the thread into the same loop as the knot in the fifth loop of the previous pyramid. Make another pyramid. The beginning thread and the working thread can be tied in a reef knot, if desired, and trimmed close to the knot.

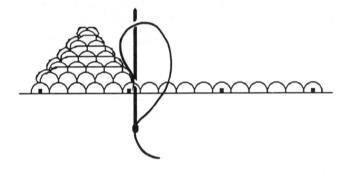

SIDE STITCH
WITH SIDE STITCH EDGING

The traditional Greek names for side stitch are *Evraiko* (Jewish stitch) or *Evraiko nero* (Jewish water stitch). The Arabic name for side stitch edging is *taj* (crown).

Worked in Butterfly crochet cotton No 50.
Finished width: 3.6 cm (1½″).

Side Stitch Pattern with Side Stitch Flower Scallop Edging

TO WORK THE SIDE STITCH PATTERN

A multiple of two is required.

- Into the first loop make a basic loop and close it with a closed loop (see instructions under closed loop and bow pattern earlier in this chapter). Miss a loop by working a large loop into the following basic loop. Repeat to the end of the round. The last large loop is worked into the first large loop.

Side Stitch Pattern

- Work a small closed loop into the same large loop, and a large loop into the next large loop. Repeat to the end of the round.

- Repeat the last round three more times.
- Work a large loop into each of the large loops.

- Onto the round of large loops, work a foundation round in a multiple of five basic loops.

TO WORK THE SIDE STITCH EDGING

A multiple of six is required.

- Miss one loop and make a large loop. Work four basic loops. Repeat to the end of the round.

- From now on, each side stitch flower is worked individually. Make a bridging loop into the large loop. Into the same loop make a small closed loop and a large loop, twice (two side stitches). Work a bridging loop into the next basic loop. Turn the work.

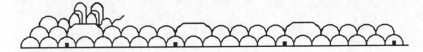

- Place the needle through the two large centre loops and work a large loop to join the two loops. Miss the bridging loop and work another large loop into the next basic loop. This will form an arch. Turn the work.

- Work two side stitches into the first loop of the arch. Make a very small bridging loop into the second loop of the arch, then work two more side stitches. Work a knot into the next basic loop, then work two more basic loops.

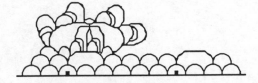 

- Repeat the second, third and fourth steps to the end of the round. Trim the thread close to the knot to finish off work.

PINEAPPLE PATTERN WITH FREE PINEAPPLE EDGING

The traditional Greek names for the small pineapple pattern are *ananas* (pineapple), *koukounara* (pine cone) or *amigthala* (almonds). The Arabic names are *ananas saghir* (junior pineapples) or *beit enahal* (beehive). Both the Greek and Arabic name for free pineapple edging is simply *ananas*, meaning pineapple.

Worked in Butterfly crochet cotton No 50.
Finished width: 3.7 cm (1½″).

Pineapple Pattern with Free Pineapple Edging

TO WORK THE PINEAPPLE PATTERN

Work a foundation round in a multiple of three. Work three rounds of basic loops.

- Miss one loop by making a large loop into the following loop. Work one basic loop. Repeat to the end of the round.

Pineapple Pattern

- Bridge into the large loop and work five long loops. Work a large bridging loop into the next large loop. Repeat to the end of the round and finish off working thread.

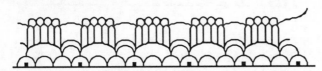

- Join the new thread at the top of the first long loop. Make a basic loop into each of the long loops. Work a large loop into the next long loop. Repeat to the end of the round.

- Repeat the last round, decreasing one basic loop each round until no loops remain.

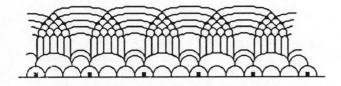

- On top of the large loops, work a foundation round in multiples of 12.
- Work six rounds of basic loops.

TO WORK FREE PINEAPPLE EDGING

A multiple of 12 is required.

Free Pineapple Edging

- Miss two loops by making a long loop into the following loop. Repeat to the end of the round.

- Into the large loop, work eight long loops. Work a large loop into the middle of the next large loop, then another large loop into the next large loop. Repeat to the end of the round. Finish off working thread.

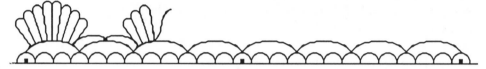

- Join the thread into the first long loop and join each long loop with a basic loop. Turn the work.

- Make a long picot into the first basic loop. Work six basic loops and turn the work.

- Repeat the last round until one loop remains. Work three long picots into the last loop. Ensure the last knot is pulled firmly. Trim the thread close to the knot.

- Join the thread into the first long loop of the next set of long loops and work the third step again. Work into the first long picot of the preceding pineapple and continue as before to complete the second pineapple. Make all the following pineapples in the same way. Join the last pineapple to the first pineapple to complete the round.

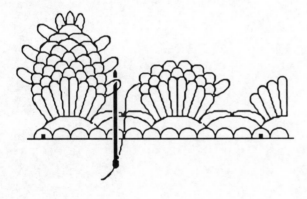

SPIRAL PATTERN
WITH BASIC FAN EDGING

The traditional Arabic names for the spiral pattern and closed loops are *kama'* (coronets) and *seeyage* (fence) respectively. Fan edging is known as *repidi* (fan) in Greek and *marwaha* (fan) in Arabic.

Worked in Butterfly crochet cotton No 50.
Finished width: 4 cm (1½″).

Spiral Pattern with Basic Fan Edging

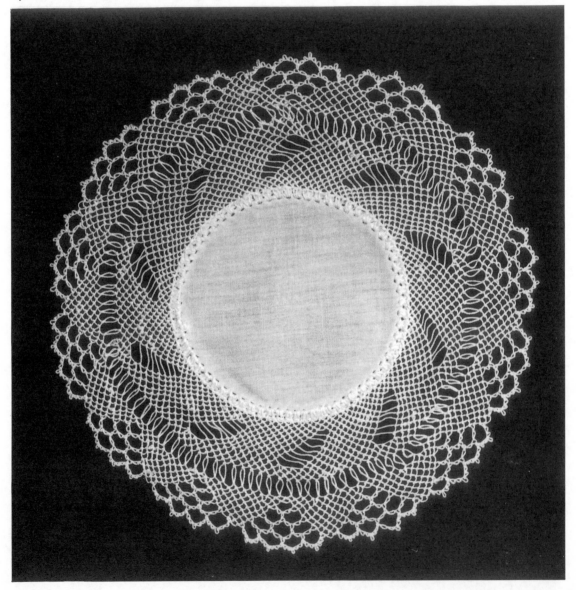

TO WORK THE SPIRAL PATTERN

A multiple of 10 is required.

- Work a foundation round in a multiple of 10.
- Miss one loop by making a large loop into the following loop. Work eight basic loops.

Spiral Pattern

- Into the large loop, work one basic loop, then work a large loop into the next basic loop. Work another seven loops.

- Repeat the last round for nine more rounds.

  Note: The large loops must increase slightly in size as the work grows or the lace will curl. If working this pattern on the straight there is no need to increase the size of the large loops.
- Onto the last round of the spiral pattern, work a foundation round of basic loops. It will be necessary to work extra basic loops into the large loops.
- Make a round of closed loops. (See instructions earlier in this chapter.)
- On top of the closed loops, work a foundation round of basic loops in multiples of 10.

TO WORK BASIC FAN EDGING

A multiple of 10 is required.

- Miss one loop by making a large loop into the following basic loop. Work eight basic loops. Repeat to the end of the round.

Basic Fan Edging

- Work a bridging loop into the large loop and make three small picots. Bridge into the next basic loop and work seven basic loops. Repeat to the end of the round.

- Miss the bridging loop and work a large loop into the middle picot. Miss the next bridging loop and work a large loop into the next basic loop. Work six basic loops. Repeat to the end of the round.

- Repeat the last two rounds until only two basic loops remain between each set of large loops.

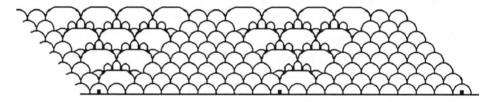

- Bridge into the large loop and work two small picots, one slightly longer picot, and two small picots. Repeat this step into the next three large loops. Bridge into the next basic loop and work one basic loop. Repeat to the end of the round. Trim thread close to the knot to finish off the work.

KNOTTED ROSE GROUND PATTERN WITH
KNOTTED ROSE GROUND DIAMOND EDGING

I have named this pattern rose ground because it resembles the bobbin lace rose ground pattern. The traditional Arabic names for rose ground and rose ground pyramids are *nejmeh* (star shape) and *kouz snobar* (pine cone), respectively.

Worked in Butterfly crochet cotton No 50.
Finished width: 6 cm (2⅓″).

Knotted Rose Ground Pattern with Rose Ground Diamond Edging

TO WORK THE KNOTTED ROSE GROUND PATTERN

A multiple of two, plus one extra loop is required.

- Work a foundation round in multiples of two plus one extra loop, then work three rounds of basic loops.
- Miss one loop by making a large loop into following loop. Repeat to the end and trim the working thread.

Knotted Rose Ground Pattern

- Join the thread into the first large loop and work two basic loops. Bridge across to the next large loop and work another two loops. Repeat to the end and trim the working thread.

- Join the thread into the first of the two basic loops and work one loop. Make a large loop into the next basic loop. Repeat to the end and trim the working thread.

- Join the thread into the basic loop. Work a bridging loop and two basic loops into the large loop. Make a bridging loop into the next basic loop. Repeat to end and trim thread.

- Repeat the last two rounds until the work is of the desired width. On the last round, work only *one* basic loop into the large loop.

- Make a round of large loops, working the knots into the basic loops of the previous round.

TO WORK KNOTTED ROSE GROUND DIAMOND EDGING

A multiple of 12 is required.

- Make a foundation round, in multiples of 12, onto the round of large loops.
- Miss two basic loops by working a large loop. Work nine basic loops. Repeat to the end of the round.

**Knotted Rose Ground
Diamond Edging**

- Into the large loop, work a bridging loop and two basic loops. Bridge into the next basic loop and work eight loops. Repeat to the end of the round.

● Make a large loop into the first of the two basic loops and work one loop. Work a large loop into the next basic loop, followed by seven basic loops. Repeat to the end of the round.

● Work a bridging loop and two basic loops into the large loop. Work a bridging loop into the one basic loop and another into the next large loop. Work two basic loops in the large loop and bridge across to the next basic loop. Work six basic loops. Repeat to the end of the round.

● Keeping the rose ground pattern correct, continue to work the pyramid, reducing the basic loops in the pyramid by one loop each round, while increasing the rose ground pattern, until only one basic loop remains on either side of the pattern.

Note: From now on the diamonds are worked individually.

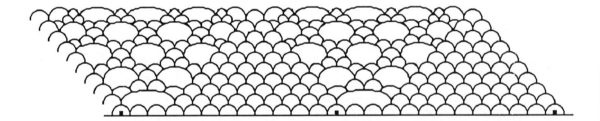

- Make a large loop into the first large loop of rose ground and keeping the pattern correct, work the rose ground pattern across to the large loop before the next pyramid.

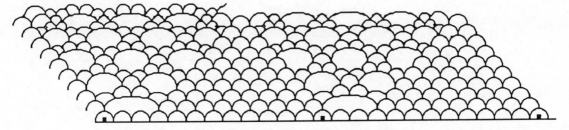

- Turn and work back to the first large loop. Turn.

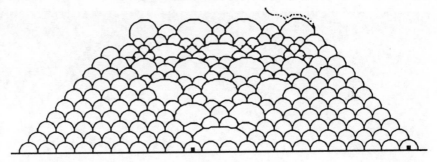

- Keeping the pattern correct, continue to work the rose ground pattern, decreasing each row by one loop to form a diamond shape. Work another large loop into the large loop at the top, then a large loop into each large loop along the right side of the pyramid and into the basic loop at the top of the next pyramid.

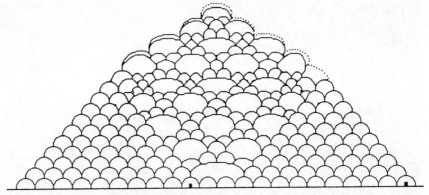

- Continue to work the next and successive diamonds in the same way.
- To complete the edging, work a round of side stitches into the loops around the top of the diamonds, ensuring that you catch both threads with the knots. Trim the thread close to the last knot to finish off work.

BELL STITCH PATTERN
WITH TUFTED PICOT FAN EDGING

Nouwar (blossom buds) is the traditional Arabic name for bell stitch, and *breem tahlab* (moss lace) is the name for tufted picot edging.

Worked in Butterfly crochet cotton No 40.
Finished width: 4.5 cm (1¾″).

Bell Stitch Pattern with Tufted Picot Fan Edging

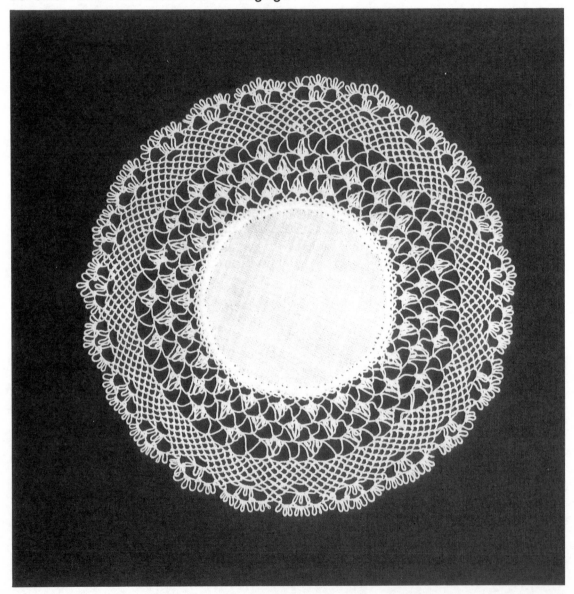

TO WORK THE BELL STITCH PATTERN

A multiple of two, plus one extra loop is required.

- Work a foundation round in a multiple of two, plus one extra loop.

- Miss one loop by making a large loop into the following loop. Work to the end, pull the knot very tight, and trim working thread.

Bell Stitch Pattern

- Join the thread in the middle of the first large loop and work a large loop and a side stitch into the next large loop.

- Bridge across to the next loop and work a small closed loop. Insert the point of the needle through the large loop of the previous side stitch and work a closed loop knot (see instructions under closed loop and bow pattern earlier in this chapter).

- Work a large loop into the same loop as the small closed loop.

- Repeat the third, fourth and last step to complete a round. Pull the knot very tight, then trim the working thread.

- Join thread at the top of a large loop and work a round of large loops into every large loop. Pull the knot very tight and trim working thread.

- Join the working thread into the loop to the left of a bell. Repeat the third, fourth and fifth steps to work another round of bells. Continue in this way until the work is of the desired width. Finish with a round of large loops.

TO WORK THE TUFTED PICOT FAN EDGING

- Onto the large loops, work a foundation round in a multiple of five.
- Work five rounds of basic loops.
- Miss one loop and work three basic loops. Repeat to the end of the round.

Tufted Picot Fan Edging

- Into the large loop, work a bridging loop and three large picots. Work a bridging loop into the next loop, then two basic loops. Repeat to the end of the round.

● Work a large loop into the first and last picot. Work a large loop into the next basic loop, then work one basic loop. Repeat to end of round.

● Work three large picots into all of the large loops. Trim thread close to knot to finish off work.

LATTICE PATTERN
WITH DAINTY PICOT EDGING

The lattice pattern has a number of traditional names. In Greek it is called *plakakia* (tiles or squares) or *baklava* (a Greek sweet of pastry and nuts cut into diamond shapes), and in Arabic, it is called *elmaz* (diamonds). The edging is called *breem tahlab* in Arabic, meaning moss lace.

Worked in Butterfly crochet cotton No 50.
Finished width: 3 cm (1⅕″).

Lattice Pattern with Dainty Picot Edging

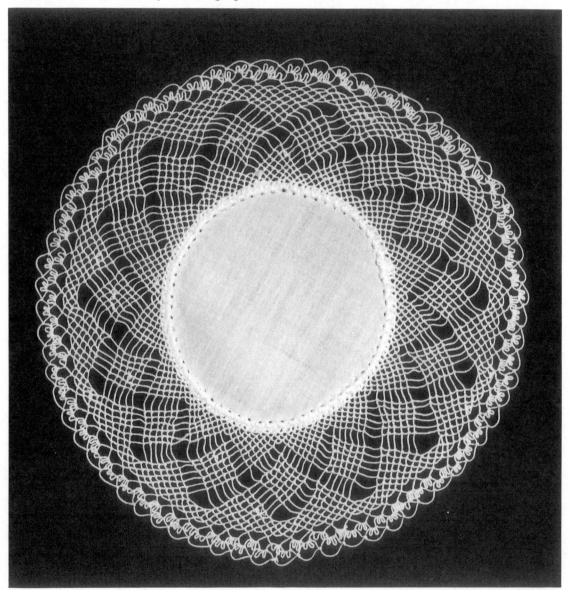

This sampler is worked in a multiple of seven. However, it can be made as large as required. Simply add more basic loops. Variations of this design can be found in Chapter 5 and in the oval doily pattern (see Chapter 6, Projects and Designs).

TO WORK THE LATTICE PATTERN

Make a foundation round in a multiple of seven and work two rounds of basic loops.

- Miss one loop by making a large loop into the following loop. Work five basic loops. Repeat to the end of the round.

Lattice Pattern

- In the next round, work a large loop into the centre of the existing large loop and then another into the next basic loop. Follow this with four basic loops. Repeat to the end of the round.

- Work a large loop into the large loop, close to the centre knot, then a basic loop into the next large loop, followed by another large loop into the next basic loop. Work three basic loops. Repeat to the end of the round.

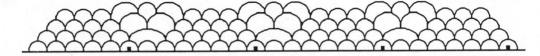

- Work a large loop into large loop, followed by two basic loops and then another large loop and two basic loops. Repeat to the end of the round.

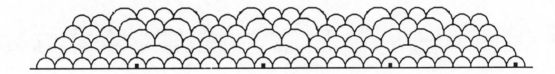

- Work a large loop into large loop, then three basic loops, another large loop followed by one basic loop. Repeat to the end of the round.

- Work a large loop into the large loop, four basic loops, then another large loop. Repeat to the end of the round.

- Work a large loop from one large loop to the next large loop, followed by five basic loops.

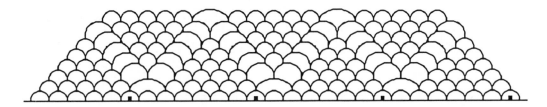

- To close the diamond design repeat the last seven steps.

- Make a foundation round of basic loops, adding extra loops into the large loops. Work four rounds of basic loops.

TO WORK THE DAINTY PICOT EDGING

A multiple of two, plus one extra loop is required.

- Miss one loop by making a large loop into the following loop. Repeat to the end of the round.

Dainty Picot Edging

- Into the large loop make two large picots. Work a large loop and two large picots into the next large loop. Repeat to the end of the round.

- Working into the large loops between picots, repeat the last step.

- To finish off, make a large loop into each large loop.

Chapter Two

MOTIF CENTRES

All samplers are worked in Butterfly crochet cotton No 50. Knotted lace doilies can be made in any shape: round, square or oval. All are started by making motif centres; that is, small rings of thread into which long, short or basic loops are worked. Four ways of beginning these centres are as follows:

Motif Centres
Anti-clockwise from top: Square centre, long loop daisy centre, small ring centre, crochet chain centre

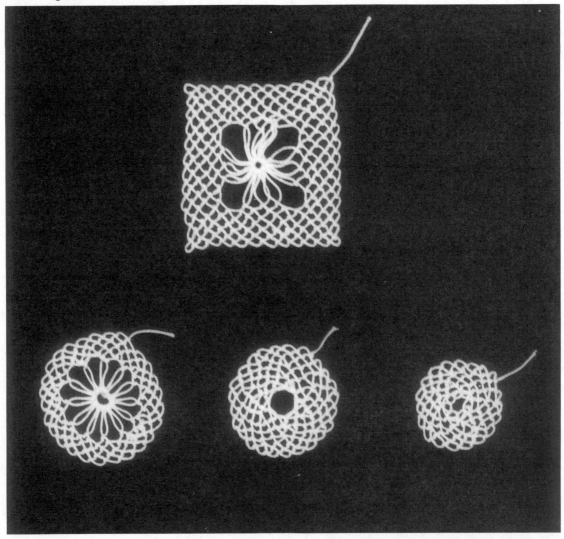

LONG LOOP DAISY CENTRE

Finished size: 2.5 cm (1″) diameter.

TO WORK THE LONG LOOP DAISY CENTRE

- Make a knot approximately 5 cm (2″) from the end of the thread. Holding the thread just above the knot, wrap it around your index finger and make a knot to join the circle.

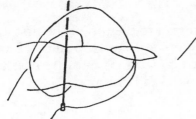

Long Loop Daisy Centre

- Into this ring, make the desired number of long loops, all of equal length. The loops will resemble a daisy.

  Note: Length and number of loops will vary according to the different patterns.

- Pull the beginning thread until the circle is the desired size. *Do not pull too tight.* Tie this thread and the working thread together in a reef knot. The working thread can be carried to the top of the first loop to continue the motif.

- Join the long loops with a round of basic loops.

THE SQUARE CENTRE

Finished size: 3.2 cm (1¼″) diameter.

TO WORK THE SQUARE CENTRE

- Make a long loop daisy centre with 12 loops.

Square Centre

- Carry the working thread to the top of the first loop and work a knot. Work a large loop into the next long loop. Make two basic loops into the next two long loops. Repeat to the end of round.

- Work three basic loops into the large loop. Make two basic loops into the next two loops and one into the next large loop. Repeat to the end of the round.

  Note: The final basic loop is worked into the first basic loop.

- Work a basic loop into the next loop and increase by one loop. This forms the corner of the square. (A small safety pin can be placed in the increased loop to mark the start of the round.) Work six basic loops, then increase again by one loop to make the next corner. Repeat to the end of the round.

- Work four more rounds, increasing at each corner every round.

SMALL RING CENTRE

Finished size: 2.2 cm (³/₄″) diameter.

TO WORK THE SMALL RING CENTRE

- Tie a thread into a half reef knot.

Small Ring Centre

- Pull to the required size and wrap the beginning thread around the circle.

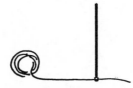

- Make six small loops into this circle, catching all the threads with the knots.

- Trim the beginning thread. Continue to work rounds of basic loops, increasing whenever necessary to keep the work flat.

CROCHET CHAIN CENTRE

Finished size: 1.7 cm ($^2/_3$″) diameter.

TO WORK THE CROCHET CHAIN CENTRE

- Crochet five chains and slip stitch into the first chain to form a ring. Cut off a length of working thread and thread through a needle.
- Make a round of basic loops into the chain.
- Make a round of basic loops, increasing whenever necessary to keep work flat.

CHAPTER THREE

MOTIFS AND MEDALLIONS

As the motif and medallion designs in this chapter are only a small sample of the many that can be created, I have included some simple as well as more complicated patterns. The instructions for some of the patterns do not have diagrams as they are easy to understand. However, before beginning any of the designs it is advisable to study the photograph of the motif or medallion you wish to work.

Motifs and Medallions
Clockwise from top centre: Long loop medallion, spiral motif, eight-pointed star motif, bibilla daisy motif, square motif, large loop and picot medallion, bibilla flower motif, raised stitch spiral motif

MOTIFS

SPIRAL MOTIF

Worked in Butterfly crochet cotton No 40.
Finished size: 8.5 cm (3⅓″) diameter.

TO WORK A SPIRAL MOTIF

- Make a long loop daisy centre with 10 long loops (see Chapter 2).

Spiral Motif

- Join the long loops with 10 basic loops.

- Work a large loop, followed by a basic loop, five times.

- Into the large loop, work another large loop followed by a basic loop. Work one basic loop. Repeat to the end of the round.

- Repeat the last step six times, increasing by one basic loop each round.

  Note: As the circle and number of basic loops increase, the size of the large loop becomes slightly smaller.

- Work six rounds of basic loops without increasing.
- Miss two loops by working a large loop into the third loop. Repeat to the end of the round.

- Into the large loop, work two small picots. Work a long picot and a small picot five times. Make another small picot, then bridge into the next large loop. Repeat to the end of the round. Trim thread.

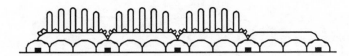

- Join the thread into one of the long picots and work a series of pineapples (four rounds). (See pineapple pattern in Chapter 1.)

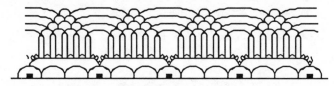

- Work a bridging loop and seven small picots into the large loop between the pineapples. Bridge into the basic loop at the top of the pineapples and work three long picots. Repeat to the end of the round.

RAISED SPIRAL MOTIF

This is a variation of the spiral motif.

Worked in Butterfly crochet cotton No 50.
Finished size: 7.5 cm (3″) diameter.

TO WORK A RAISED SPIRAL MOTIF

- Work the first three steps of spiral motif (described at the beginning of this chapter).
- Into the large loop, work another large loop and a basic loop. Into the next basic loop, work a raised stitch (see beginning of Chapter 6). Repeat to the end of the round.

Raised Spiral Motif

- Into the large loop, work a large loop and two basic loops. Into the next basic loop make a raised stitch. Repeat to the end of the round.

- Repeat this last step five times, increasing the number of basic loops each round.

  Note: The raised stitch is worked into the loop to the *left* of the raised stitch of the previous round.

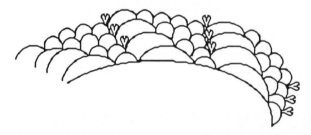

- Work six rounds of basic loops, including the raised stitch.
- Continue as for the spiral motif.

SQUARE MOTIF

Worked in Butterfly crochet cotton No 40.
Finished size: 7.5 cm (3″) square.

TO WORK A SQUARE MOTIF

- Start with a square centre (see Chapter 2), and work two rounds of basic loops, increasing by one loop at each corner.
- Work a round of bows (see closed loop and bow pattern in Chapter 1). Ensure that a complete bow is worked into each corner loop.

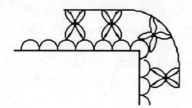

Square Motif

- On top of the bows, work a foundation round of basic loops.
- Work five rounds of basic loops.
- Make another round of bows as in the second step.
- Work another three rounds of basic loops.
- Finish the square motif by working the large loop and picot edging (see Chapter 1).

BIBILLA MOTIF

Worked in Butterfly crochet cotton No 50.
Finished size: 5.5 cm (2⅙″) diameter.

TO WORK A BIBILLA MOTIF

- Make a loop daisy centre with 17 long loops (see Chapter 2).
- Join the large loops with basic loops. There should be 17 basic loops.
- The petals are made individually in the following manner.
- Work two basic loops. Turn and work a large loop into the first basic loop. Turn work and increase one loop into first loop. Work one loop and increase one loop into the same loop. Ensure that you catch the thread of the large loop with the knots.

Bibilla Motif

- Turn work and work a large loop into the first loop. Turn work and increase one loop into the first loop. Work two loops and increase one loop. There should now be four loops.

- Repeat the second row twice, increasing by one loop each row. There should be six loops.

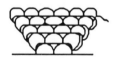

- Turn and make a large loop into the first loop. Turn and work five basic loops.

- Repeat the last row, decreasing by one loop each row until only one loop remains.

- Work into last loop, and down the left side of the petal to the middle of the petal. Leave a workable length of thread when trimming working thread.

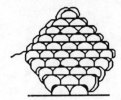

- Join thread into next basic loop and work another bibilla petal. Work down the middle of the petal and join it to the right side of the previous petal. Trim thread close to the knot.

- Work six more petals.
- Using the thread left on the first petal, join it to the last petal. Trim the thread close to the knot.

MEDALLIONS

LARGE LOOP AND PICOT MEDALLION

Worked in Butterfly crochet cotton No 50.
Finished size: 5 cm (2″) diameter.

TO WORK A LARGE LOOP AND PICOT MEDALLION

- Start with a small ring centre (see Chapter 2), and work nine rounds of basic loops. Increase the number of loops each round to keep the work flat. Ensure that there is an even number of loops in the final round.
- Miss one loop by making a large loop. Repeat to the end of the round.
- Into each large loop, work five small picots.
- Weave the thread through the first two picots and work into the middle picot. Work a large loop into the middle picot of next group of picots. Repeat to the end of the round.
- Into the first large loop, work four very small picots, three larger picots and another four very small picots. Bridge into next large loop. Repeat this step to the end of the round. Trim the thread close to the knot.

LONG LOOP MEDALLION

Worked in Butterfly crochet cotton No 50.
Finished size: 5 cm (2″) diameter.

TO WORK A LONG LOOP MEDALLION

- Start with a small ring centre (see Chapter 2), and work three rounds of basic loops, increasing until there are 12 basic loops.
- Work two long closed loops (see Chapter 1) into each basic loop.
- Work a round of basic loops, in multiples of three, on top of the long closed loops.
- Miss one loop and work a large loop. Make a basic loop into next loop. Repeat to end of round.
- Into the large loop, work five small picots. Bridge into the basic loop and work three longer picots. Repeat to end of round.

POINTED STAR MOTIF

Worked in Butterfly crochet cotton No 60.
Finished size: 4.5 cm (1¾″) diameter.

- Make a 12-looped daisy centre.
- Begin at the top of one large loop and work a bibilla petal (see the bibilla daisy motif, this chapter). Work three more petals in the same manner.

Pointed Star Motif

- Join the working thread into the right-hand long loop at the base of one of the petals and work a large loop across to the next long loop. Turn and work three small picots into the large loop.

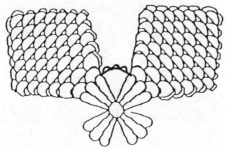

- Work two small loops up the right-hand side of the first petal, then work a large loop into the middle picot. Work another large loop into the third row of the next petal. Turn and work three picots into each of the large loops, with a small bridging loop between.

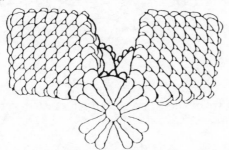

- Work another two small loops up the side of the petal and work two large loops into the middle picots, and another large loop into the sixth row of the next petal. Turn and work three picots into each of the large loops, with small bridging loops between.

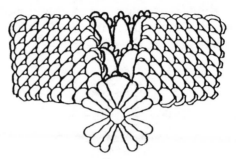

- Turn the work and weave the working thread through the first picot and make a knot into the middle picot. Work two large loops into the next two middle picots. Turn and work three picots into the large loops, with a small bridging loop between.

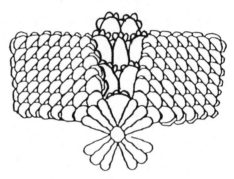

- Turn and weave through the first picot and make a knot into the middle picot. Work one large loop. Turn and work three picots into this loop. Trim thread to finish off work.

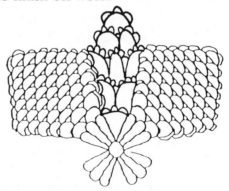

- Repeat from the third step to the last step to complete the motif.

BIBILLA FLOWER

Worked in Butterfly crochet cotton No 30.
Finished size: 5 cm (2″) diameter.

TO WORK A BIBILLA FLOWER

- Make a long loop daisy centre with 16 loops (see Chapter 2).
- Join each loop with a basic loop. Work two more rounds of basic loops.
- Miss one loop and work a large loop into the next loop. Repeat to the end of the round. There should be eight large loops.
- Into the first large loop work five basic loops. Work a bibilla pyramid onto these loops (see Chapter 1).
- Work down the left side of pyramid and trim the working thread.
- Join the thread into the next large loop and make another bibilla pyramid. Work down the left side of pyramid and tie the working thread and the joining thread in a reef knot. Trim threads close to the knot. Work a bibilla pyramid into each of the remaining large loops.

CHAPTER FOUR

CORNERS, EDGINGS AND INSERTIONS

All of the edgings described in this book can be used as trimmings for anything which requires a lace edging. Permanent trimmings can be worked directly onto hemmed or neatened edges of fabric. Removable trimmings can be started in one of two ways:

- **The crochet chain footing,** where the lace is worked onto a crochet chain, the length of the item to be trimmed.
- **Double thread footing,** where the lace is worked onto a double strand of thread the length required.

Note: Both the crochet chain and the double thread footing can be slipstitched onto the edge to be trimmed and the lace worked as normal. Be careful when working the foundation row that the knots do not catch the slip stitches or the fabric, as this will make lace difficult to remove when required.

Clockwise from top right: Flower edging, three-loop pyramid edging, floral fan edging, bow and picot edging

CORNERS

It is not always possible to have completely square corners when working lace edgings. To ensure that the corners are neat and even, place the centre of the fan, scallop or other pattern on the corner of the work. This can be done by starting and counting the basic loops of the foundation round at a corner.

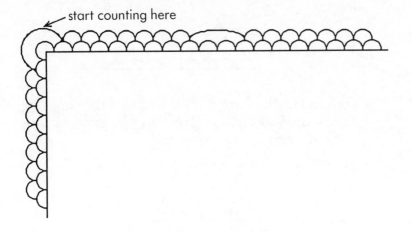

start counting here

Corners

HORIZONTAL EDGINGS

THREE-LOOP PYRAMID EDGING

Worked in Butterfly crochet cotton No 50.
Finished width: 1.8 cm (¾″).

TO WORK THREE-LOOP PYRAMID EDGING

● Work a foundation row or round in a multiple of five basic loops.

   Note: If this edging is being worked onto a square, the third loop in the set of five should be placed directly on the corner.

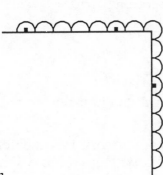

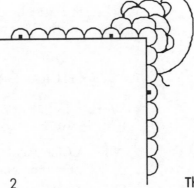

1

2

Three-loop Pyramid Edging

- Work three basic loops. Turn and work a large turning loop and two more loops.

- Turn and work a large turning loop and one basic loop.

- Turn and work a large turning loop into the remaining basic loop. Make a large loop into the next basic loop on the foundation row or round.

- Repeat the second, third and fourth steps until the end of the round or row.

FLORAL FAN EDGING

Worked in Butterfly crochet cotton No 50.
Finished width: 1.8 cm (¾″).

TO WORK FLORAL FAN EDGING

- Work a foundation row or round in multiples of 10 basic loops.

  Note: When working a square, work in a multiple of 10, plus nine additional basic loops. Situate a fan on the corners.

- Miss two loops by working a large loop into the following loop. Work seven basic loops. Repeat to the end of the row or round.

  Note: If turning a corner, it is only necessary to miss one basic loop.

Floral Fan Edging

- Into the large loop, work a large bridging loop and a basic loop. Work another long bridging loop into the next basic loop. Make six basic loops. Repeat to end of row or round.

- Miss the bridging loop and work a large loop into the basic loop. Work another large loop into the next basic loop. Make five basic loops. Repeat to the end of the row or round.

- Work a large bridging loop and a basic loop into first large loop. Bridge into the next loop and work another basic loop. Work another large bridging loop into the next basic loop. Make four basic loops. Repeat to the end of the row or round.

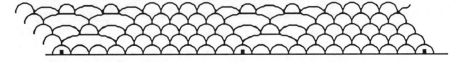

- Missing the bridging loops, work large loops into the next three basic loops. Work three basic loops.

  Note: The middle large loop is slightly smaller than the other large loops. If working around a corner, the large loops of the fan will need to be larger than the large loops worked on the straight.

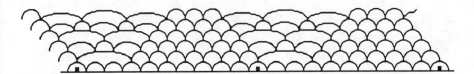

● Bridge into the first large loop and work four small picots. Work a small bridging loop and five long picots into the next large loop. Bridge into the next large loop and work four small picots. Work a bridging loop into the next basic loop, then work two more basic loops. Repeat to the end of the row or round.

Note: When working a corner fan, work seven small picots into the first and third large loops and seven long picots into the middle large loop.

● Miss all the small picots and work a large loop into the first long picot. Work a basic loop into each of the four long picots. Work another large loop into the next basic loop. Make one basic loop. Repeat to the end of the row or round.

Note: When working a corner fan, the large loops will need to be larger than those on the straight.

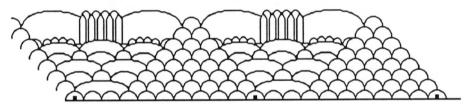

● Bridge into the first large loop and work five small picots. Bridge into the first basic loop and work a side stitch. (See Chapter 1.) Work a side stitch into the next three basic loops. Bridge into the next large loop and work five small picots. Work a bridging loop into the one basic loop. Repeat to the end of the round.

Note: When working a corner fan, work nine small picots into the first loop and six side stitches into the basic loops on top of the long picot.

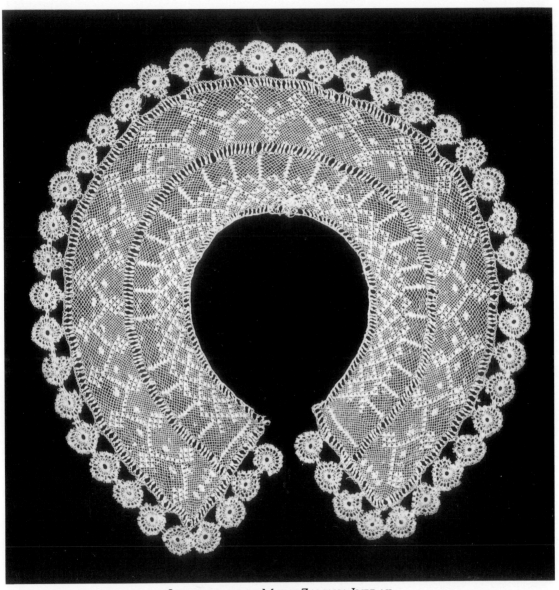

LACE COLLAR BY MARIE ZAMAKA JUBRAIL
Made in very fine crochet cotton, as part of her trousseau. Circa 1912.
Finished width 10.75 cm.

DOILY BY ASPASIA BAMBACAS
Worked in fine crochet cotton, this doily was made by Aspasia for her granddaughter. Circa 1970. Finished size 38 cm diameter.

ROUND DOILY BY EIRENE DIMETRIOU DICKSON
Made in a very fine crochet cotton. Circa 1940. Finished size
44.5 cm diameter.

DOILY WITH WOVEN THREAD DESIGN BY EIRENE DIMETRIOU DICKSON
Circa 1940. Finished size 25 cm diameter.

DOILY BY EIRENE DIMETRIOU DICKSON
One of a set of three made for her son. Circa 1950.
Finished size 33.5 cm diameter.

OVAL DOILY BY KATOA'A JALEELEH
This doily from Palestine was made by Katoa'a as part of her daughter's
trousseau. Circa 1954. Finished size 42.5 cm long by 27.5 cm wide.

DOILY DESIGNED AND MADE BY ANGELLIKY TOPALSAVAS
Worked in fine crochet cotton. Circa 1939. Finished size 30.5 cm from
point to point.

SQUARE DOILY BY ASPASIA BAMBACAS
Worked as part of her trousseau. The centre design has been worked by
weaving embroidery floss through the loops. Circa 1930.
Finished size 31 cm square.

DOILY BY ASPASIA BAMBACAS
Worked in very fine cotton. Circa 1930. Finished size 50.5 cm diameter.

DOILY BY ASPASIA BAMBACAS
Worked in fine crochet cotton, this doily was made by Aspasia for her
granddaughter. Circa 1970. Finished size 41.5 cm diameter.

DOILY BY ASPASIA BAMBACAS
Worked in fine crochet cotton, this doily was made by Aspasia for her
granddaughter. Circa 1970. Finished size 37.5 cm diameter.

SQUARE DOILY BY ANGELLIKY TOPALSAVAS
Comprised of small motifs, this doily was designed and made by
Angelliky for her niece. Each motif is 9 cm in diameter. Finished size of
doily is 26 cm square.

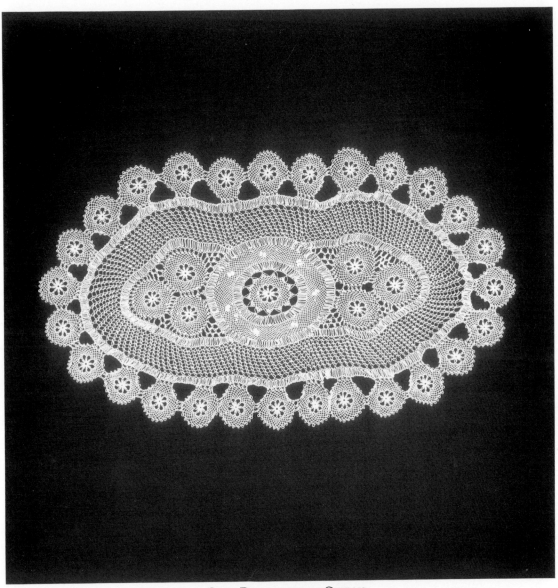

OVAL DOILY MADE IN CYPRUS
Finished size 48.5 cm long by 27.5 cm wide.

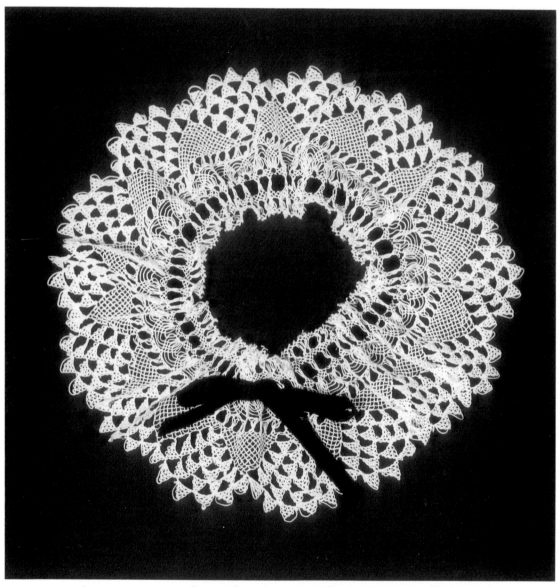

LACE EDGING FOR A PAIR OF PANTALOONS BY EIRENE DIMETRIOU DICKSON
Worked in a very fine cotton, as part of her trousseau. Circa 1930.
Finished width 9 cm.

ROUND DOILY BY EIRENE DIMETRIOU DICKSON
One of a set of three made for her son. Worked in No. 50 crochet
cotton. Circa 1966. Finished size 31 cm diameter.

ROUND DOILY BY EIRENE DIMETRIOU DICKSON
Worked in No. 30 Butterfly cotton, this doily was made by Eirene for
her grandson. Circa 1979. Finished size 35.5 cm diameter.

FLOWER EDGING

Worked in Butterfly crochet cotton No 50.
Finished width: 1.8 cm (¾″).

TO WORK FLOWER EDGING

- Work a foundation row or round in a multiple of eight basic loops. Each flower is worked individually from now on.
- Miss two basic loops by working a large loop. Turn work and make another large loop over the previous large loop, working the knot over the previous knot.

Flower Edging

- Catching both threads of the large loops with the knots, work three very small picots and a long picot three times. Work three more small picots and work a very small bridging loop into the same basic loop as the large loop. Work one basic loop.

- Turn work and join the three long picots with large loops. Miss one basic loop by working another large loop into the following basic loop.

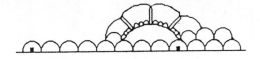

- Turn work. Into the first large loop work four small loops. On these loops work a small bibilla pyramid. (See Chapter 1.)

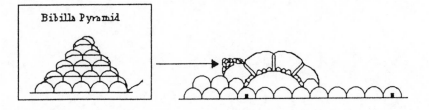

Bibilla Pyramid

- Work down the right side of the pyramid to the next large loop. Make four more bibilla pyramids spacing them evenly across the next three large loops. Work down the right-hand side of the last pyramid into the large loop, and bridge across to the next basic loop.

- Work three basic loops and repeat the last four steps. Join the top of the pyramid to the top of the last pyramid before making the remaining pyramids.

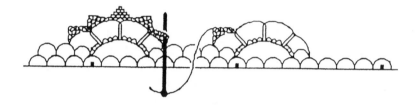

- Repeating the last six steps, make flowers to the end of the row or round. If working around a square or circle, join the last pyramid to the very first pyramid before finishing off the thread.

VARIATION OF FLOWER EDGING

Substitute the bibilla pyramids with three-loop pyramids.

BOW AND PICOT EDGING

Worked in Butterfly crochet cotton No 50.
Finished width: 1.7 cm (²/₃″).

TO WORK BOW AND PICOT EDGING

- Work a foundation row or round in a multiple of two basic loops.
- Make a row or round of bows onto the foundation loops. (See Chapter 1.)

  Note: If working a corner, work a complete bow into the corner loops.

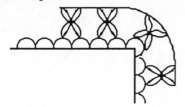

Bow and Picot Edging

- On top of the bows, work a foundation row or round in a multiple of three, and then work one row or round of basic loops.

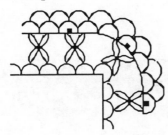

- Miss one loop by working a large loop into the following basic loop. Work one basic loop. Repeat to end of row or round.

  Note: When working a corner, ensure that the large loops are situated on the corners, and miss two (not one) basic loop.

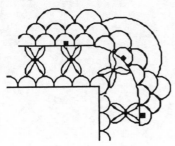

- Bridge into the large loop and work three picots. Work a bridging loop into the one basic loop. Repeat to the end of the row or round.

Note: More picots may need to be worked into the large corner loop.

VERTICALLY WORKED EDGING

Worked in Butterfly crochet cotton No 50.
Finished width: 4 cm (1$\frac{1}{2}$″).

Vertically Worked Edging

TO WORK VERTICALLY WORKED EDGING

- Make a crochet chain or double thread footing (see the beginning of this chapter), and work 10 basic loops. If you find it difficult to work with the small footing, slip stitch it to a scrap of fabric until the lace is long enough to handle easily.

- Turn and make a small turning loop into the first loop. Miss one loop by making a large loop. Repeat four times. Work one basic loop. Turn the work.

- Work a turning loop into the basic loop. Make a basic loop and two picots into the first large loop. Work a bridging loop and three picots into each of the next three loops (2). Make a loop into the base of the first large loop and close it at the top (3). (This creates a footing edge for the lace.) Turn the work.

- Work a smaller large loop into the middle picot of the previous round. (Half loop made.) Make a large loop into the next two middle picots and into the second picot of the next group of picots. Work two basic loops, then work another basic loop into the last loop. Turn the work.

- Into the first basic loop work a long picot and a basic loop. Work two basic loops. Into the first large loop work one basic loop and two picots. Work a bridging loop and three picots into the next two large loops and a bridging loop and two picots into the half loop. Work down into the base of the large loop and close the loop. Turn the work.

● Miss the picots of the half loop and work a large loop into the next two middle picots. Work a large loop into the second picot of the next group of picots, then work four basic loops. Make another basic loop into the last loop. Turn the work.

● Continue in this way until there are 13 basic loops and one large loop. Turn the work.

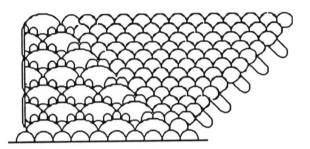

● Work two long picots into the first basic loop. Make 12 basic loops. Into the large loop work a bridging loop and three picots. Work a loop into the base of the previous row and close it. Turn the work.

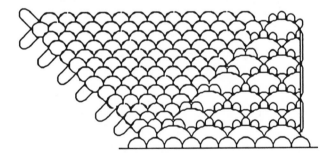

● Work a half loop into the second picot. Miss one picot and the bridging loop and work a large loop into the next loop. Work 11 basic loops. Turn the work.

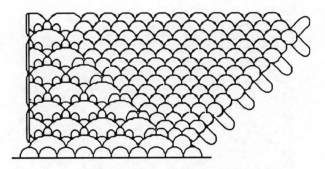

● Work a long picot into the first basic loop. Make 10 basic loops, then a bridging loop and two picots into the large loop. Work two picots into the half loop. Work down into the base of the half loop and close the loop. Turn the work.

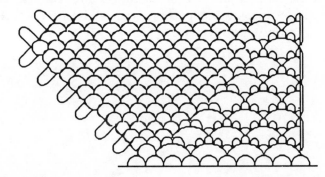

● Miss the picots in the half loop and work a large loop into the second picot of the next loop. Miss one loop by making a large loop into the next basic loop. Work nine basic loops. Turn the work.

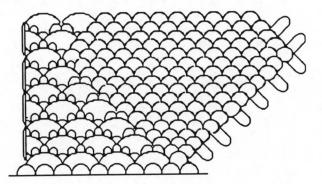

- Continue in this manner, decreasing the number of basic loops until there are four large loops and one basic loop.

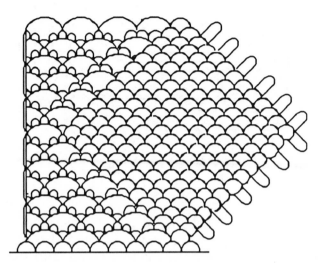

- Repeat the last 10 steps until the lace is the length required. If desired, designs can be woven into the basic loop diamond pattern with white or coloured embroidery cotton.

INSERTIONS

This lace is ideal for joining two pieces of fabric in a decorative manner. The simplest method is to work a row of long closed loops (see Chapter 1) along the edge of one piece of fabric, then slip stitch the second piece of fabric to the top of the closed loops. Alternatively, a row of bows (see Chapter 1) can be worked and slip stitched in the same way as the closed loops. If the closed loops and bows are long enough, ribbons can easily be threaded through them. More decorative insertions can be created by using a variety of other patterns.

Top row: Rose ground pattern used to join two pieces of fabric, and a rose ground insertion
Middle Row: Closed loops used to join two pieces of fabric, and lattice edging
Bottom Row: Basic loops and bows used to join two pieces of fabric and a flower edging variation

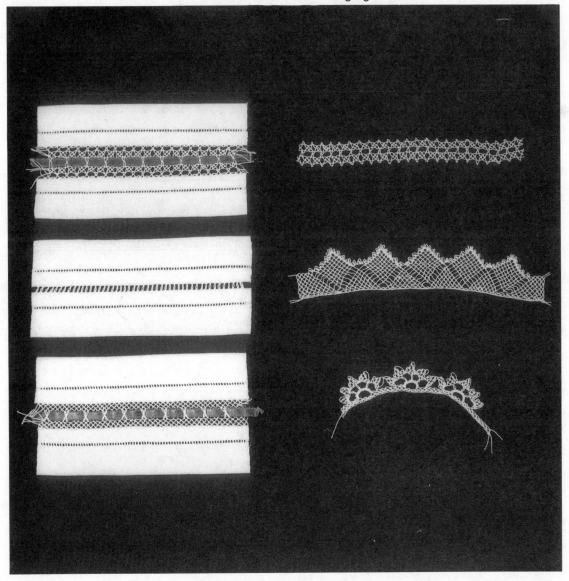

KNOTTED ROSE GROUND PATTERN

The knotted rose ground pattern is a more decorative insertion that is especially useful for this purpose.

TO WORK THE KNOTTED ROSE GROUND
PATTERN INSERTION

- Work a foundation row in a multiple of two, plus one basic additional loop, along the edge of one piece of fabric. Trim the thread at the end of each row and join again at the left side of the work.

- Miss one loop by working a large loop into the following loop. Repeat to the end of the row.

Knotted Rose Ground Insertion

- Join the thread into the large loop and work two basic loops. Bridge into the next large loop. Repeat to the end of the row. Trim the thread and join it into the first basic loop.

- Work one basic loop into the next basic loop and a large loop into the next basic loop. Repeat to the end of the row. Trim the thread and join it into the end basic loop.

- Work a large bridging loop and a long picot into the large loop. Work another large bridging loop into the basic loop. Repeat to the end of the row. Trim the thread.

Note: The length of the picot can be varied to suit your particular purpose.

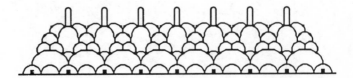

- On the second piece of fabric, work the first four steps again.
- To join the two edges, work the bridging loop into the large loop. Hold both pieces of lace together, wrong sides touching, and place the needle through the long picot and work a knot. Work another knot into the large loop. Work a bridging loop into the next loop.

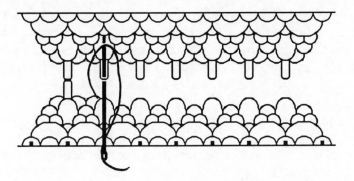

- If desired, the basic loops in which the large loops are worked can be cut to make a length of insertion. Ribbon can be threaded between the joined picots.

CHAPTER FIVE

EXTENDED CORNERS

Not all patterns are suitable for extended corners. Fans, pineapples, scallops or any pattern which spreads or flares during working should not be used. The most effective patterns to use are those explained in this chapter as well as large loop and picot, side stitch, knotted rose ground, bell stitch and lattice (all of which are described in Chapter 1).

Extended Corners
Clockwise from top right: Large loop and picot corner with feathered picot fan edging; picot lattice pattern with a fancy closed loop scallop edging; bell stitch corner with long loop and side stitch edging and three picot pattern corner with closed loop and picot fan edging

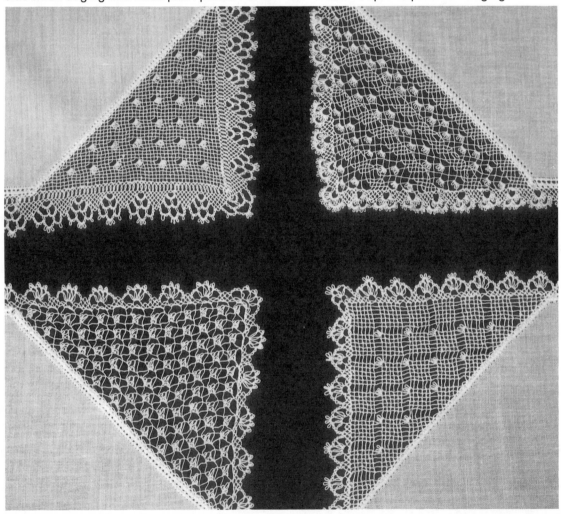

The lace edgings described in this chapter can be used on any edging. When working a square *always* situate a fan or scallop on each corner.

Note: It is advisable when working an edging around an extended corner not to begin the edging on the lace corner.

PICOT LATTICE PATTERN WITH A FANCY CLOSED LOOP AND PICOT SCALLOP EDGING

Worked in Butterfly crochet cotton No 50.
Finished size: 14.5 x 10.5 cm (5¾ x 4⅐").

This is a variation of the lattice design described in Chapter 1.

TO WORK A PICOT LATTICE CORNER

- Work a foundation row in a multiple of eight, plus seven additional basic loops. Turn and work a small turning loop.

  Note: Do not work into the small turning loops.
- Work six basic loops. Miss one loop by working a large loop into the following loop. Repeat to the end of the row. Turn and work a small turning loop.

Picot Lattice Corner

- Continue to work the lattice design as explained in Chapter 1 for five rows.

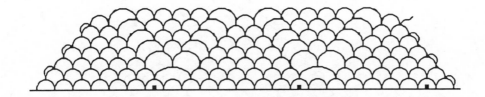

- Turn work and make a small turning loop. Make a large loop into the large loop. Work four basic loops. Into the one basic loop work a large loop and then three long picots. Repeat to the end of the row.

- Turn and work a small turning loop into the large loop. Work a large loop and five basic loops. Work a large loop over the three picots. Repeat to end of row. Turn the work and make a long turning loop into the large loop.

- Repeat the last four steps to close the lattice pattern. Continue to work the pattern in this way until one basic loop remains. Trim the thread close to the knot to finish off work.

TO WORK FANCY LOOP AND PICOT SCALLOP EDGING

Finished width of edging 1.3 cm ($\frac{1}{2}''$).

- Work a foundation round or row in a multiple of six.
- Miss one loop by working a large loop. Work four basic loops. Repeat to the end of the round or row.

    Note: When working a corner, ensure that a large loop is situated on the corner.

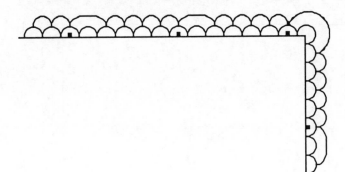

Fancy Closed Loop and Picot Scallop Edging

- Miss the basic loop before the large loop and work a large loop and close it. Work three more long closed loops. Miss the next basic loop and work another large loop. Work one basic loop. Repeat to the end of the round or row.

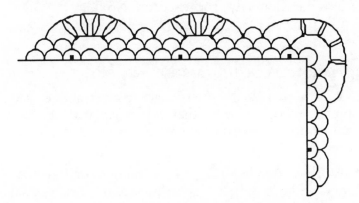

- Bridge into the large loop and work five small picots across the top of the first two closed loops. Between the second and third closed loops work three long picots. Work five small picots across the next two closed loops. Bridge into the one basic loop. Repeat to the end of the round or row. Trim the thread close to the knot to finish off the work.

BELL STITCH CORNER WITH LONG LOOP AND SIDE STITCH SCALLOP EDGING

Worked in Butterfly crochet cotton No 50.
Finished size: 14.5 x 10.5 cm (5³/₄ x 4¹/₇″).

TO WORK BELL STITCH CORNER

This is a particularly pretty lace corner and is very simple to work. Ensure that you begin with an even number of large loops which will give an uneven number of bells.

- Work a foundation row in a multiple of four, plus one additional basic loop. Turn and work a small turning loop into the first loop.
- Miss one loop by making a large loop into the following loop. Repeat to the end of the row. Turn the work.

Bell Stitch Corner

- Work a large loop into the first large loop, and then work a row of bells as explained in Chapter 1 (see bell stitch pattern).

- Turn work and make a large turning loop into the top of the first bell. Work a row of large loops across the top of the bells.

- Turn work and make a long turning loop into the first large loop. Work a large loop into the next large loop. Make a row of bells into the large loops to the end of the row. Turn and work a large turning loop.

- Repeat the last two rows until only one bell remains. Trim the thread close to the knot to finish off the work.

TO WORK THE LONG LOOP AND SIDE
STITCH SCALLOP EDGING

Finished width: 1.3 cm (½″).

- Work a foundation row or round in a multiple of
  seven basic loops.
- Miss one loop by working a large loop. Work five
  basic loops. Repeat to the end of the round or row.

  Note: When working around a square, ensure that
  a large loop is situated on each corner.

**Long Loop and
Side Stitch Scallop Edging**

- Miss the basic loop prior to the large loop and work
  a large loop, and close it. Work three more long
  closed loops. Miss the next loop and work a large
  loop into the next basic loop. Work two basic loops.
  Repeat to the end of the round or row.

- Bridge into the first large loop and work three small
  picots. Into the next three loops work a bridging loop
  and a side stitch into the next three loops. Into the
  large loop work a bridging loop and three small
  picots. Bridge into the next basic loop and work one
  loop. Repeat to the end of the row. Trim the thread
  close to the knot to finish off the work.

THREE PICOT CORNER WITH CLOSED LOOP AND PICOT FAN EDGING

Worked in Butterfly crochet cotton No 50.
Finished width: 13 x 9.2 cm (5 x 3½").

TO WORK A THREE PICOT CORNER

- Work a foundation row in a multiple of seven basic loops. Turn and work a small turning loop into the first loop.
- Work one row of basic loops. Turn and work a small turning loop into the first loop.
- Work five basic loops. Miss one loop by working a large loop into the following loop. Repeat to the end of the row.

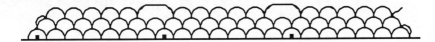

Three Picot Corner

- Turn and work a small turning loop. Work four basic loops. Make a basic loop and three long picots into the large loop. Work four basic loops. Repeat to the end of the row.

- Turn and work a small turning loop into the first basic loop. Work four basic loops. Make a large loop over the three picots, then work five basic loops. Repeat to the end of the row.

• Turn and work a small turning loop into the first loop. Work three basic loops. Make two basic loops into the large loop, then one into the next basic loop. Work four basic loops. Repeat to end of row, finishing with four basic loops. Turn the work and make a small turning loop into the first basic loop.

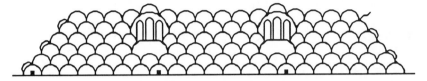

• Work a row of basic loops. Turn and work a small turning loop into the first basic loop.

• Repeat the last row.

• Continue to repeat the last seven rows until one loop remains. Trim the thread close to the knot to finish off thread.

TO WORK CLOSED LOOP AND PICOT FAN EDGING

Finished width: 2 cm (³/₄″).

• Work a foundation row or round of basic loops.

• Work a closed loop into each of the basic loops.

   Note: When working around a corner, three closed loops are worked into the corner loop.

Closed Loop and Picot Fan Edging

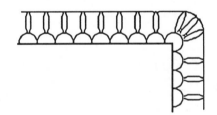

• On top of the closed loops, work a foundation row, or round, in a multiple of eight.

• Miss one loop by making a large loop. Work six basic loops. Repeat to end of row or round.

● Bridge into the large loop and work two small picots, one long picot and two more small picots. Bridge into the next loop, then work five basic loops.

● Work a large loop into the long picot and another into the next basic loop. Work four basic loops. Repeat to the end of the row or round.

● Bridge into the first large loop and work two small picots, one long picot and one small picot. Work a bridging loop into the next large loop and work one small picot, one long picot and two small picots. Make a bridging loop into the next basic loop and work three basic loops. Repeat to the end of the row or round.

● Join the two long picots with large loops and work another large loop into the next basic loop. Work two basic loops. Repeat to the end of row or round.

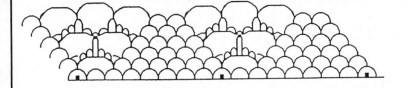

- Bridge into the first large loop and work two small picots, one long picot and one small picot. Bridge into the next large loop and work one small picot, three long picots and another small picot. Bridge again and into the third large loop work one small picot, one long picot and two small picots. Bridge into the next basic loop and work one loop. Repeat to the end of the row or round. Trim the thread close to the knot to finish off work.

LARGE LOOP AND PICOT CORNER WITH FEATHERED PICOT FAN EDGING

Worked in Butterfly crochet cotton No 50.
Finished size: 14 x 10 cm ($5\frac{1}{2}$ x 4").

TO WORK A LARGE LOOP AND PICOT CORNER

- Work a foundation row in a multiple of five, plus four additional basic loops. Turn the work and make a small turning loop into the first loop.
- Work three basic loops. Miss one loop by making a large loop. Repeat to the end of the row.

Large Loop and Picot Corner

- Turn the work and make a small turning loop into the first basic loop. Make two basic loops. Work one basic loop into the large loop, then a large loop into the next basic loop. Repeat to the end of the row, finishing with two basic loops.

- Turn the work and make a small turning loop into the first basic loop. Work one basic loop. Make a large loop into the right-hand side of the large loop. Work three basic loops. Repeat to the end of the row.

- Turn the work and make a small turning loop into the first basic loop. Work two basic loops. Make a basic loop into the large loop, then a large loop into the next basic loop. Repeat to the end of the row.

- Turn the work and make a long turning loop into the large loop. Miss one loop by making a large loop. Repeat to end of the row. Work a basic loop into the last loop. Turn the work and make a small turning loop into the first basic loop.

- Into the first large loop work one basic loop and three long picots. Make a large loop into next large loop. Work another large loop and three long picots into the next large loop. Repeat to the end of the row. Work a basic loop into the large loop of the previous row.

● Turn the work and make a small turning loop into the first basic loop. Work a row of large loops into each of the large loops. Make the final loop into the basic loop after the three picots.

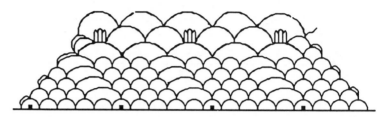

● Turn the work and make a turning loop into the first large loop. Work a large loop and three picots into the next large loop. Make one large loop into the next loop. Repeat to the end of the row. Turn the work and make a turning loop into the first large loop.

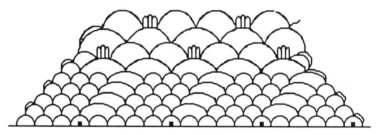

● Work a large loop into each large loop. Turn the work and make a turning loop into the first large loop.

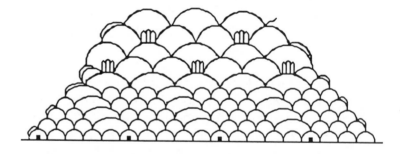

● Repeat the last 10 steps until only one large loop remains. Trim the thread close to the knot to finish off work.

TO WORK FEATHERED PICOT FAN EDGING

Finished width: 1 cm ($1/3''$).

- Work a foundation row or round in a multiple of six basic loops.
- Work four basic loops, miss one loop by working a large loop. Work another four basic loops. Repeat to the end of the row or round.

  Note: When working a square, the large loops must be situated on the corner.

Feathered Picot Fan Edging

- Into the large loop, work a bridging loop, three long picots, one small picot and three long picots. Bridge into the next loop and work three basic loops. Repeat to the end of the row or round.

- Miss the three picots and work a large loop into the small picot. Make another large loop into the next basic loop. Work two basic loops. Repeat to the end of the row or round.

- Into the first large loop, work a small bridging loop, three long picots, one small picot and three long picots. Bridge into the next large loop and repeat the three long, one small and three long picots. Work a bridging loop into the next basic loop and make one basic loop. Repeat to the end of the row or round. Trim the thread close to the knot to finish off work.

CHAPTER SIX

PROJECTS AND DESIGNS

FILLED DESIGNS

Filled designs can be worked in one of two ways:

- By using two or three long picots to fill the loop.

- By working a raised stitch, ie, working a closed loop and a basic loop into the loop to be filled.

As I prefer to use the second method, all my instructions will refer to raised stitches.

Many varied patterns can be worked using either of these methods. By photocopying the pages of basic loops at the end of this chapter you can create your own designs. Alternatively, graph paper placed diagonally can be used.

Before attempting any of the complicated filled designs in this book, it is advisable to work the following bookmark.

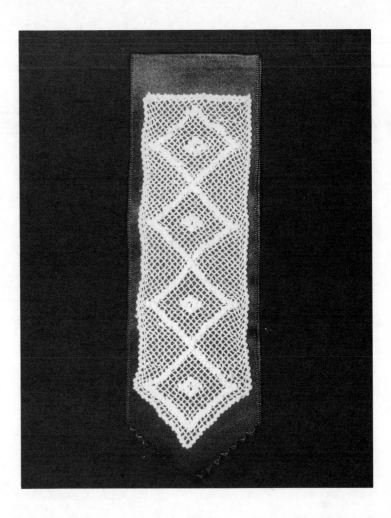

Bookmark featuring a
Filled Diamond Design

DIAMOND DESIGN BOOKMARK

Worked in Butterfly crochet cotton No 40.
Finished size: 14.75 x 5.75 cm ($5^3/_4$ x $2^1/_4$").

Note: To keep edges straight be sure to work into the
turning loop each row.

TO WORK THE BOOKMARK

- Make a base by using either the double thread or
  chain footing (see Chapter 4), and work 19 basic
  loops. Turn the work.

Bookmark

- Work a turning loop into the first loop, then work nine basic loops. Into the same loop as the last knot, work a raised stitch. Work nine basic loops. Turn the work.

- Work a turning loop into the first loop, followed by eight basic loops. Make a raised stitch into the same loop as the last knot. Work one loop, then another raised stitch. Work nine basic loops. Turn the work.

- For the next eight rows continue to work the raised stitches, decreasing the number of basic loops at the sides of the bookmark, and increasing the basic loops between the raised stitches.

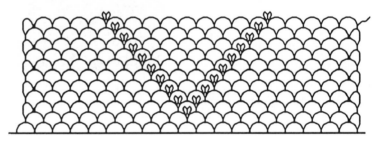

- Work a turning loop into the first loop followed by four basic loops and one raised stitch. Make five basic loops. Into the same loop as the last knot work a raised stitch. Work five basic loops, then another raised stitch. Work to the end of the row. Turn the work.

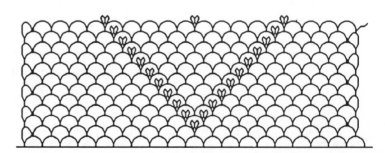

- Work a turning loop into first loop, followed by three basic loops and a raised stitch. Work five basic loops and one raised stitch. Make another basic loop and a raised stitch. Work five basic loops and a raised stitch. Make four basic loops. Turn the work.

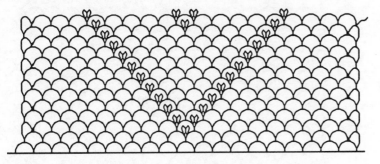

- Make a turning loop into first loop. Work three basic loops and a raised stitch. Work five basic loops and a raised stitch, followed by two basic loops and a raised stitch, then five basic loops and a raised stitch. Work three basic loops. Turn the work.

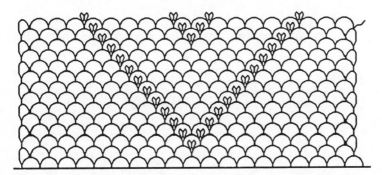

- Work a turning loop into the first loop, then three basic loops. Work a raised stitch into the same loop as the last knot. Make five basic loops and another raised stitch. Work one basic loop, followed by a raised stitch and five basic loops. Work another raised stitch, then four basic loops. Turn the work.

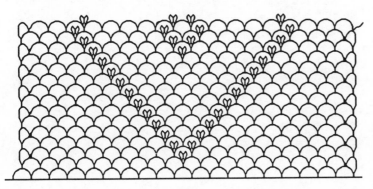

- Continue to work in this manner until the small and large diamond design is complete.

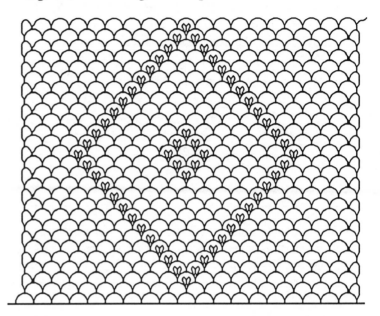

- Work one row of basic loops before repeating the second to the last steps to make another diamond design.

- When the lace is the required length, work a pyramid while closing the diamond design.

  Note: The pyramid is formed by working a small turning loop at the beginning of each row. This loop is *not* worked into.

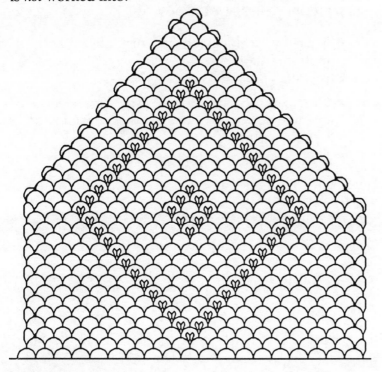

- To finish off the bookmark, work small picots all the way around the lacework.
- If using the raised stitch to work the filled pattern, decide which side of the lace is the right side and, with the point of the needle, hook all the raised stitches to the right side.

  Note: When working in the round, the raised stitches will always be on the right side.

ROUND DOILY WITH FILLED DESIGN

Worked in Butterfly crochet cotton No 50.
Finished size: 48.5 cm (19″) diameter.

TO WORK THE ROUND DOILY

- Begin by working the first nine steps of the spiral motif in Chapter 3.
- Join the pineapples with large loops.
- On top of these large loops, work a foundation round in multiples of two, and work six rounds of basic loops.
- Make a round of bows (see Chapter 1).

Round Doily featuring a spiral motif, bows, filled zig-zag, spot, diamond and pine tree designs with a filled pyramid edging

ZIG-ZAG PATTERN

- On top of the bows, work another foundation round in a multiple of six basic loops. Following the diagrams below, work the zig-zag pattern.

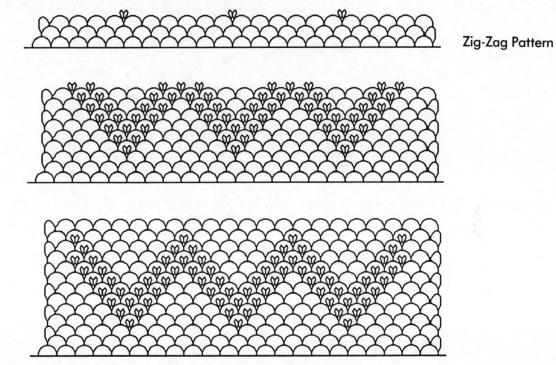

Zig-Zag Pattern

- On top of the zig-zag design, make a round of bows as in the fourth step of the round doily pattern (see above). Work a foundation round in a multiple of two on top of the bows and work four rounds of basic loops. Work another round of bows on top of these loops.

SPOTS PATTERN

- Work a foundation round in a multiple of six and, following the diagrams below, work the spots pattern.

Spots Pattern

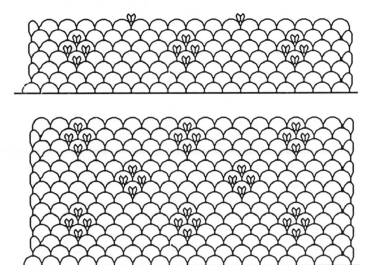

- Repeat the last step of the zig-zag pattern.

DIAMOND PATTERN

- Work a foundation round in a multiple of six and, following the diagrams below, work the diamond pattern.

Diamond Pattern

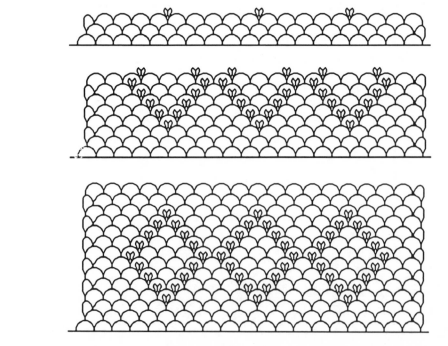

- Finish by repeating the final step of the zig-zag pattern.

PINE TREE PATTERN

- Work a foundation round in a multiple of nine. Following the diagrams below, work the pine tree pattern.

  Note: As the diameter of the work increases, so must the size of the loops or the work will curl.

- Finish by repeating the final step of the zig-zag pattern.

Pine Tree Pattern

FILLED PYRAMIDS

- Work a foundation row in a multiple of 25 and, following the diagram below, work the filled pyramids.

  Note: Each pyramid is worked individually. Finish off the thread at the top of each pyramid.

Filled Pyramids

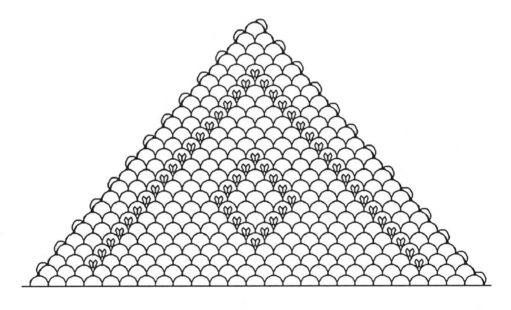

- Around the edge of the pyramids, work the three-loop pyramid edging described in Chapter 4.

SQUARE DOILY WITH FILLED BUTTERFLY DESIGN
AND BASKET STITCH FAN EDGING

Worked in Butterfly crochet cotton No 60.
Finished size: 23 cm (9″) square.

TO WORK A SQUARE DOILY

● Work a square centre (see Chapter 2) and work seven
rounds of basic loops.

Note: There should be 10 basic loops between each
corner loop.

Square Doily featuring a filled butterfly design and basket stitch edging

- Work bows (see Chapter 1) around the square.

  Note: Into the corner loops, work the last leg of the previous bow, one complete bow and the first leg of the next bow.
  Between each corner bow there should be six bows.

Square Doily

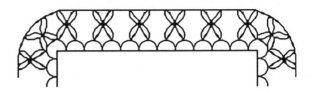

- On top of the bows, work a round of basic loops.

  Note: A corner loop must be worked on top of the corner bow.
  There should be 14 basic loops between each corner loop.

- Work six rounds of basic loops, increasing at each corner until there are 17 basic loops between each corner loop.

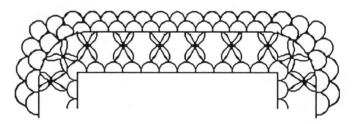

BUTTERFLY DESIGN

- Following the chart, work the butterfly pattern for the next 30 rounds.

  Note: Remember to increase at each corner.

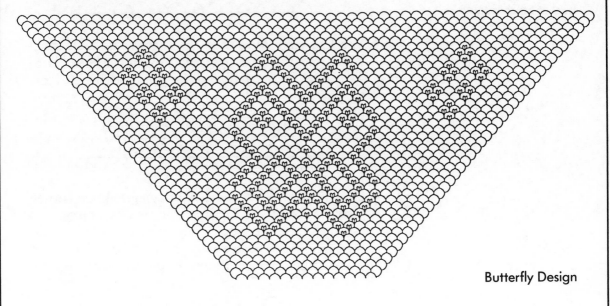

Butterfly Design

- Work six more rounds of basic loops.
- Work a round of bows onto the basic loops as in the second step (Bows).

  Note: There should be 29 bows between each of the corner bows.

BASKET STITCH EDGING

- A multiple of 21 basic loops is required if working a straight edge.
- Work a foundation round of basic loops on top of bows.

  Note: There should be 61 basic loops between each corner loop.

- Start the edging one loop before a corner. Across each side of the square miss the corner loop and make a large loop. *Work 18 basic loops, miss two loops and make a large loop*. Repeat from * to * once more, then work 18 more basic loops.
- Repeat the last step around the remaining three sides of the square.

- Make a bridging loop into the large loop and work three picots. Bridge into the next basic loop and work 17 basic loops. Repeat to the end of the round.

Basket Stitch Edging

- Work a large loop into the first picot, then small loops into the next two picots. Work another large loop into the next basic loop followed by 16 basic loops.

- Into the large loop, work a bridging loop and three picots. Work two loops into the next two picots and one into the large loop. Make three more picots into the large loop. Bridge into the next basic loop and work 15 basic loops. Repeat to the end of the round.

- Keeping pattern correct, continue the last two steps until one basic loop remains.

  Note: When working on a straight edge, the fan flares out. This means that the large loops next to the basic loop pyramid will need to decrease each round. Therefore, by the second to last round, the large loops will need to be about the size of a basic loop. The corners will need to fan out more; therefore, the large loops will need to be enlarged.

- To work the picot edging around the basket stitch fan, begin at a corner fan. Miss the first basket and work a large loop into the middle picot of the group of three picots. Repeat this once more. Around the corner of the fan, work a large loop into the middle picot of the basket stitch and one into the middle picot of the group of three picots eight times. Miss the next basket and work a large loop into the middle picot of the next group of three picots, then a large loop into the remaining basic loop.

- Work across the straight section of the square by working a large loop into the third picot of each set of three picots.

- Repeat the last two steps around the remaining three sides of the square.

- Into each large loop, work a bridging loop, two small picots, three long picots and two more small picots. Finish off thread.

- To work the picot edge around the basket stitch fan, work two small, three long and two small picots into each large loop. Trim the thread close to the knot to finish off the work.

OVAL DOILY

Worked in Butterfly crochet cotton No 50.
Finished size: 34.5 x 28 cm (13½ x 11″).

Most oval-shaped doilies are begun by joining three or more small motifs or medallions. The more motifs, the longer the oval.

Once these motifs are joined, the spaces between them must be filled by using leaves, bows, closed loops, large loops and picots, or any other technique which complements the motifs.

Oval Doily comprising three centre motifs, bows, column pattern, lattice with bows pattern and a filled lattice and diamond pattern edging

TO WORK AN OVAL DOILY

The foundation round for the next pattern is worked on top of whichever method is used to join the motifs.

Note: To maintain the oval shape it is necessary to increase the number of loops only at the oval ends of the doily.

If too many loops are worked into the straight edge the work will frill and eventually take on a round shape.

CENTRE MOTIFS

- Make a daisy centre with 18 long loops, and join them with basic loops.

Centre Motifs

- Work two rounds of basic loops.

- Into the next loop work two picots.
- Work a basic loop and two picots into every loop to the end of the round.

- Into each basic loop between the picots, work a large loop.

- Work a bridging loop into the first large loop and make three picots. Repeat to the end of the round and trim off thread.

- Make another motif by repeating the first five steps above. Join it to the first motif by working three picots into the first large loop. Bridge into the next large loop and work one picot. Place the wrong sides of each motif together and place the needle through the middle picot of the first motif and make a basic knot. Work into the large loop of the second motif to complete the second picot. Work one more picot, then bridge into the next large loop. Repeat the process with the next group of picots, thus joining the motifs in two places. Continue to work a bridging loop and three picots into each large loop to finish the second motif. Trim the thread.

- Make another motif and join it to the second motif in the same way as the first. Trim the thread.

- Join the thread into one of the middle picots and work a round of closed loops around all three motifs. Into the large spaces between the motifs, work large bows.

- On top of the closed loops, work a foundation round in a multiple of two and work seven rounds of basic loops.

  Note: Add more loops around the ends of the oval than on the straight edges.

- Work a round of bows on top of the basic loops (see Chapter 1).

COLUMN PATTERN

- Work a foundation round in a multiple of 10.
- Into the next loop, work one basic loop and a side stitch, ie, a small closed loop and one large loop. Bridge into the next loop and work another side stitch, and eight basic loops. Repeat to the end of the round. Work into the loop prior to the side stitch.

Column Pattern

- Place the needle through the front of the two large loops and work a large loop. Work another large loop into the next basic loop, followed by seven basic loops. Repeat to the end of the round.

- Into the first large loop, work one basic loop and one side stitch. Make a bridging loop into the next large loop and make another side stitch. Work seven basic loops and repeat to the end of the round.

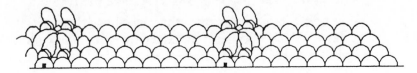

- Repeat the last two rounds however many times are necessary to complete the desired number of rounds. Finish with the first of those two rounds.
- Work a round of basic loops in a multiple of two, plus one extra loop.

  Note: Add extra loops into large loops.
- Work a round of bows on top of the basic loops.

LATTICE DESIGN WITH BOWS

- On top of the bows, work a foundation round in a multiple of seven.
- Miss one loop and make a large loop into next loop. Work five basic loops. Repeat to the end of the round.
- Work a large loop into the centre of the large loop and another into the next basic loop. Work four basic loops. Repeat to the end of the round.
- Place the needle under both large loops and make a loop. All loops will join in the centre. Make another loop into the corner of the large loop of previous round (bow made).

Lattice Design with Bows

- Make a basic loop into next large loop. Place the needle under the two large loops and make another bow. Work into the next three basic loops.

- Repeat the last two steps to complete the round.
- Work a large loop into the right-hand loop of the bow. Work two basic loops followed by a large loop and two basic loops. Repeat to the end of the round.

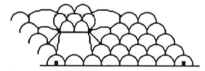

- Work a large loop into the large loop close to the basic loops. Work three basic loops and another large loop and one basic loop. Repeat to the end of the round.

- Place the needle under two large loops, as for the fourth step above and make another bow. Work four basic loops, then make another bow, working into the one basic loop.

- Work a large loop across to the right-hand side of the next bow, then work five basic loops. Repeat to the end of the round.

- Repeat the third step to the last step to complete the lattice pattern. Repeat these steps until the pattern is the desired width.

- Onto the last row of lattice with bows pattern, work a foundation round in a multiple of two.

   Note: When working basic loops into the large loops, put more into the loops around the oval ends.

- Work a round of bows as in the third step.

FILLED LATTICE AND DIAMOND EDGING

A multiple of 14 basic loops is required.

This edging is a half lattice design pattern with a pyramid on top to create a diamond effect. Each pyramid is worked separately. The filled design is worked with raised stitches (see instructions at the beginning of this chapter). Follow the graph for their placement each round.

- Work a foundation round in multiples of 14 basic loops.
- Miss one loop by working a large loop and one basic loop. Into the next loop work a basic loop and a raised stitch (see instructions at the beginning of this chapter). Work seven basic loops, followed by a basic loop and a raised stitch into the next loop. Make two basic loops. Repeat to the end of the round.

Filled Lattice and Diamond Edging

- Work a large loop into the large loop and the next basic loop. Into the next loop, work one basic loop and a raised stitch. Work six basic loops, then into the next loop, work another loop plus a raised stitch. Work two more loops and repeat to the end of the round.

- Work a large loop into the first large loop, a basic loop into the next large loop and a large loop into the next basic loop. Work one basic loop. Make a basic loop and raised stitch into the next loop. Work two basic loops, then a basic loop and a raised stitch into the next loop. Work two loops. Repeat to the end of the round.

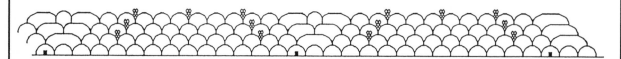

- Continue in this manner for 10 more rounds. Be careful to follow the pattern diagram to ensure the correct placement of raised stitches.

- Make a large loop into next large loop and, following the diagram, work across to next large loop. Repeat to the end of the round.

- Each of the lattice diamonds is worked individually. Following the graph for placement of raised stitches, work across to next large loop. Turn and work a small turning loop.

  Note: This loop is not worked into next row.

- Following the diagram for placement of raised stitches, work the rest of the pyramid, decreasing each row until one basic loop remains. Finish off the thread.

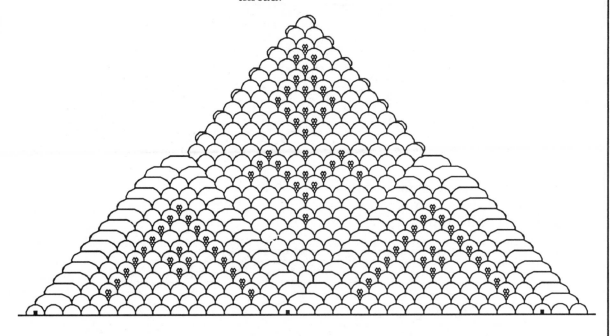

- Join the thread into the next large loop close to the basic loops and work another filled pyramid. Repeat to the end of the round.
- Around the edges of the pyramids work a round of bows.

  Note: Into basic loop at the top of each pyramid, work a three-legged bow, ie, work two long closed loops and then join them with the third closed loop.

Bows

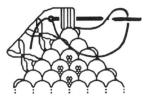

- On top of the bows, work a round of side stitches. Into each three-legged bow, work seven long loop picots.

SPIRAL DOILY

Worked in Butterfly crochet cotton No 30.
Finished size: 23 cm (9″) diameter.

TO WORK A SPIRAL DOILY

- Begin with a long loop daisy centre containing 21 loops. Join the loops with basic loops and work another round of basic loops.

  Note: There should be 22 basic loops. Add one extra if necessary.

Spiral Doily: Original pattern by Katoa' a Jaleeleh, courtesy of her daughter Nina Jubrail

- Into each basic loop work a bow (see Chapter 1).
  Note: There should be 22 bows.

Spiral Doily

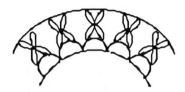

- Work 45 basic loops on top of the bows.
- Miss one loop by making a large loop, then work three basic loops. Repeat to the end of the round.

- Work a large bridging loop into the large loop followed by three small loops, then three basic loops. Repeat to the end of the round.

- Miss the bridging loop and work a large loop into the second small loop, followed by four basic loops. Repeat to the end of the round

- Repeat the last two steps nine times and then the first of the last two steps once more.
- Miss the bridging loop and work a large loop into the second small loop, miss one loop and work another large loop into the next loop. Work 12 basic loops. Repeat to the end of the round.

- Continue as for basic fan edging (see Chapter 2), finishing with a round of picots into large loops. Trim the thread.
- Locate the loop above the basic loop pyramid. Into the second middle picot to the left of this loop, join a thread and work a large loop into the middle picot of the next four sets of picots. Turn the work.

Join thread here

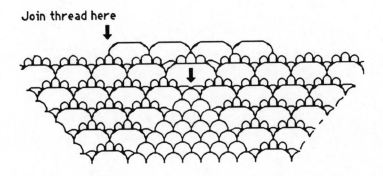

- Work three picots into three large loops and two picots into the fourth. Turn and work a large loop into each middle picot. Turn the work.

- Repeat the last row until one large loop remains. Picot into this large loop and down the left side of the looped pyramid. Tie the working thread and joining thread with a reef knot and trim ends.

- Join the thread into the same picot as the last long loop of first row of looped pyramid, and repeat the last three steps until there are looped pyramids all the way around the work.

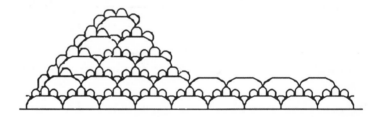

LACE COLLAR WITH *FLEUR DE LIS* PATTERN AND CLOSED LOOP AND PICOT SCALLOP EDGING

Worked in Butterfly crochet cotton No 50.
Finished width: 8.5 cm ($3\frac{1}{3}$").

Many very pretty collars can be made by using any of the patterns, or combination of patterns, in this book. They are worked in the same way as horizontal lace edgings and the work must be turned at the beginning of each row. The lace is usually worked onto a crochet chain or double thread footing, the length of the neckline. If the pattern used does not flare or increase while the work grows, it will be necessary to insert a pattern which will increase the number of loops.

Lace Collar comprising of a *fleur de lis* pattern with a closed loop and picot scallop edging

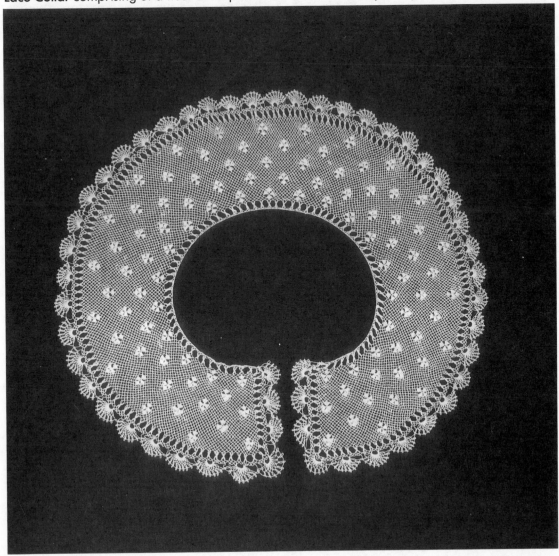

TO WORK THE COLLAR

- Prepare a crochet chain or double thread footing the length of the neckline (see Chapter 4). Onto the footing, work a foundation row of basic loops in a multiple of two. Turn and work a small turning loop into the first basic loop.
- Work a row of bows onto the foundation row (see Chapter 1). Turn the work.
- On top of the bows, work a foundation row in a multiple of seven basic loops.

TO WORK THE *FLEUR DE LIS* PATTERN

A multiple of seven loops is required.

- Make a turning loop into the first loop. Into the next loop, work one basic loop and a side stitch (see Chapter 1).
- Into the next loop, work a small bridging loop and another side stitch.

Fleur de Lis Pattern

- Work six basic loops. Into the same loop as the last knot, work a side stitch. Bridge into the next loop and work another side stitch. Repeat to the end of the row. Turn and work a turning loop into the first loop.

- Place a needle through the front of the larger loops of the two side stitches and join them with a large loop. Work a large loop into the next basic loop.

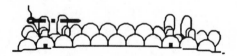
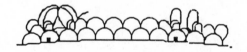

- Work five basic loops. Join the next two side stitches with a large loop, as in the previous step. Make another large loop into the next basic loop. Repeat to the end of the row. Turn and work a turning loop into the first loop.

- Into the large loop, work a basic loop and two side stitches.
- Into the next large loop, work a bridging loop and another two side stitches. Work five basic loops. Repeat the last two steps to the end of the row.

- Turn work and work a turning loop into the first loop. With a large loop, join the first two side stitches. Make a large loop into the bridging loop between the side stitches. Join the next two raised stitches with another large loop. Work five basic loops. Repeat to the end of the row.

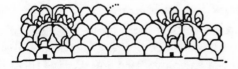

- Turn and work a small turning loop into the first loop. Into the large loop, work one basic loop. Work a basic loop and a side stitch into the next large loop. Bridge into the next large loop and work a side stitch. Make a basic loop into the next loop. Work five basic loops. Repeat to the end of the row.

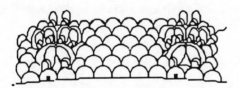

- Turn and work a small turning loop into the first loop. Work one basic loop. Join the two side stitches with a large loop. Work a large loop into the next basic loop. Work seven basic loops. Repeat to the end of the row.

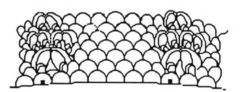

- Turn and work a small turning loop into the first loop. Work a basic loop into each loop to the end of the row. Do not work into the small turning loop.
- Repeat the last step.
- Repeat the last step again, only remember to work into the turning loop at the end of the row. Turn and work a turning loop into the first loop. Work four basic loops.
- Into the next loop, work a basic loop and a side stitch. Bridge into the next loop and work another side stitch. Work seven basic loops. Repeat to the end of the row. Turn and work a turning loop into the first loop and work five basic loops.
- Join the side stitches with a large loop. Work a large loop into the next basic loop. Make seven basic loops. Repeat to the end of the row. Turn and work a turning loop into the first loop. Work four basic loops.
- Into the first large loop, work a basic loop and two side stitches. Work a basic loop and two side stitches into the next large loop. Make seven basic loops. Repeat to the end of row. Turn and work a turning loop and five basic loops.
- Join the two side stitches with a large loop. Work a large loop into the basic loop between the side stitches. Join the next two side stitches with a large loop. Work a large loop into the next basic loop, followed by seven basic loops. Turn and work a turning loop into the first loop. Work four basic loops.
- Work a basic loop into the first large loop. Into the next large loop, work a basic loop and a side stitch.

Bridge into the next large loop and work a side stitch. Work a basic loop into the next large loop, followed by seven basic loops. Repeat to the end of the row. Turn and work a turning loop and six basic loops.

- Join the two side stitches with a large loop. Make another large loop into the next basic loop. Work nine basic loops. Repeat to the end of the row.

- Turn and work a turning loop into the first basic loop. Work a basic loop into each loop to the end of the row.

- Repeat the last row twice.

- Repeat all of the above 21 steps until the collar is of the desired width. Finish off the thread.

    Note: The number of basic loops between the *Fleur de lis* pattern will increase as the work grows, allowing the collar to flare.

- With the right side of the collar upwards, join the thread into the bow on the left side of the work and make a row of bows (see Chapter 1) around the edge of the collar. When turning a corner, work a complete bow into the corner loop.

TO WORK CLOSED LOOP AND PICOT SCALLOP EDGING

A multiple of eight loops is required.

- With the right side of the collar upwards, join the thread on top of the bow at the left side of the work, and work a foundation row of basic loops down to the first corner in a multiple of eight, plus four additional loops. Ensure that the eighth loop is situated on the corner. Continue to work the foundation row across to the next corner in a multiple of eight. Again, the eighth loop must be on the next corner. Work the remaining loops in a multiple of eight, plus four extra loops along the side of the collar to the neck edge. Finish off the working thread.

- Join the thread into the first basic loop and work three basic loops. Make a large loop by missing a loop and working into the following loop.

Closed Loop and Picot Scallop Edging

- Turn the work and make another large loop into the same loop as the previous knot.

- Turn the work and bridge into the large loop with a very small loop and work nine long loops. Work another bridging loop into the base of the large loops and another two basic loops.

- Turn the work and make a large loop into the first long loop and join each long loop with a basic loop. Miss two basic loops and work a large loop into the first basic loop.

- Turn the work and make a long closed loop into the first basic loop between the long loops.

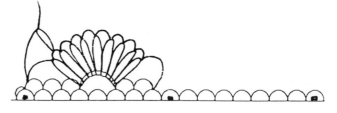

- Place the needle under the knot of the closed loop and work a picot.

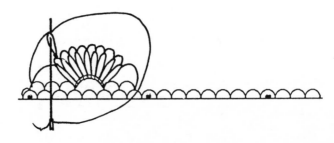

- Make a closed loop and picot into each of the basic loops between the long loops, and one into the large loop. Work a large loop down into the next basic loop on the foundation row.

- To make the next scallop, repeat the first five steps. Join the second scallop to the first by placing the needle through the front of the last picot and working a long loop. Continue to make closed loops and picots as for first scallop.

- Complete the edging by working the remaining scallops in the same way as the second scallop. Trim thread close to knot to finish off work.
- A fine ribbon can be threaded through the bows at the neckline.

Page of Basic Loops for Photocopying

REFERENCES

ANCHOR, *Manual of Needlework*. B.T. Batsford Ltd, London, 1968.

CHURCHILL-BATH, Virginia, *Lace*. Penguin, Harmondsworth, 1979.

KASPARIAN, Alice Odian, *Armenian Needlelace and Embroidery*. E.P.M. Publications, McLean, Virginia, 1983.

SIMEON, Margaret, *The History of Lace*. Stainer and Bell, London, 1979.

YANNARA, Tatiana Ioannou, *Greek Threadwork Collection of Laces*. Melissa, Athens, 1986 (Greek language).

PHOTOGRAPHY CREDITS

For the wooden tray and paperweight
(appearing in Plate 1):
David Ireland Needlecraft
4/2-4 Kepple Drive
Hallam Vic 3803

For the doll's house chair
(appearing in Plate 6):
Mrs Margaret Morgan
Thumbelina
7 Gilmore Road
Henley Beach Road
SA 5022
(07) 356 3437

For the doll's bed
(appearing in Plate 6):
Doll's House Gallery
237 Anzac Highway
Plympton SA
(07) 371 0433